passover by design

picture-perfect kosher by design® recipes for the holiday

By Susie Fishbein

Photography by John Uher

Published by ARTSCROLL / SHAAR PRESS
4401 Second Avenue / Brooklyn, NY 11232 / (718) 921-9000
www.artscroll.com • www.kosherbydesign.com

Distributed in Israel by SIFRIATI / A. GITLER
6 Hayarkon Street / Bnei Brak 51127 / Israel

Distributed in Europe by LEHMANNS
Unit E, Viking Business Park, Rolling Mill Road
Jarrow, Tyne and Wear, NE32 3DP / England

Distributed in Australia and New Zealand by GOLDS WORLD OF JUDAICA
3-13 William Street / Balaclava, Melbourne 3183, Victoria / Australia

Distributed in South Africa by KOLLEL BOOKSHOP
Shop 8A Norwood Hypermarket / Norwood 2196 / Johannesburg, South Africa

ISBN-10: 1-57819-073-8 / ISBN-13: 978-1-57819-073-7

Printed in the USA by Noble Book Press

DEDICATION

The publication of this book marks the first Passover since the death of my mother-in-law **MYRNA FISHBEIN** ל"ז. "Muth's" warmth, generosity, and graciousness helped make her a wonderful hostess for many years of *sedurim* and other memorable occasions. Her table always sparkled and the food and conversation flowed. Yet Muth always kept in mind a point that I have made in all my cookbooks. Never lose sight of why you are going through all the effort, and of the family and friends for whom you are doing it.

This point is best brought home through a story from my husband's childhood. While playing baseball in the yard, his mitt broke and there was an urgent need to immediately replace such an important item. He came running in to ask his mother to take him to a special store about a half-hour away to buy a new one. This, however, was no regular day. It was the day of the first seder and she was busy preparing. Without missing a beat, she took him to that store and got him just the right mitt — and the seder was still spectacular.

When he got older, my husband realized how cool this was of her and how it demonstrated her ability to get so much done while keeping a smile on her face. While the mitt wore out over time, the memory never did. He still has that mitt as a keepsake and the story has a special place in our hearts. This book is dedicated to her memory and in gratitude for all the memories she created for us.

THANK YOU

It is with gratitude to Hashem that I am blessed to be writing yet another thank-you page.

The beauty is in the details and my team understands details. It is with tremendous appreciation that I thank: Gedaliah Zlotowitz, the ArtScroll Family, John Uher, Melanie Dubberley, Renee Erreich, Larry Sexton, Moshe David, Endo Kazuhito, Lito Tan, Tzini Fruchthandler, Eli Kroen, Elisa Greenbaum, Karen Finkelstein, Lorena Barrios, Elizabeth Parson, and Felice Eisner. Your skills, style, and perfectionism always exceed my highest expectations.

Thank you to: Atlas Floral Decorators for the gorgeous and generous flowers.

Aharon Kaplan of Tiferes Matzah in the Five Towns for out-of-season shmura matzo.

Michael Strauss Silversmiths for the gorgeous Judaica.

McCabe's Wine and Spirits for the wine.

And of course to my husband Kalman and my kids Kate, Dani, Jodi, and Eli. I may provide the meals but you provide the moments we savor.

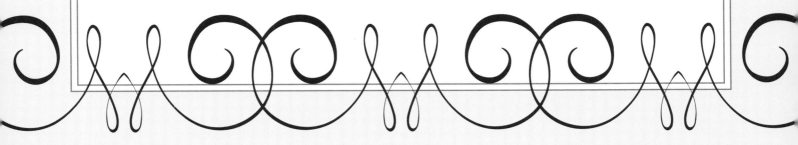

Some of my best childhood memories revolve around Passover. My parents hosted every year. My aunt and uncle would pull up in our driveway about two hours before sundown. An army of helpers would unload their sea of aluminum foil to join my Mom's ocean of aluminum foil and this would kick off the action. My Grandma would man the frying pan, whipping up "chremsil" or pancakes for anyone in her path. My good-hearted cousins would grab my brother and head out to the deck to grate the maror. My other grandmother would lead my cousins, my sister, and me to the green plastic bowl to prepare the charoset. One of us worked the silver nutcracker to crack the walnuts, while another on the mezzaluna furiously chopped apples. We'd grab a spare relative as taste tester to decide if we needed more wine. My dad would be organizing Shabbos clocks and sleeping arrangements, which would mean sleeping bags under the dining room table when necessary. The simple seder table that stretched the length of my house was set as we awaited the arrival of my other cousins as well as beloved neighbors and friends. My parents wouldn't have traded this organized chaos for anything; and it still resonates with me all these years later. That is the beautiful thing about making holidays at home — they become precious memories etched on us and our children.

Yet hosting the seder strikes fear into the hearts of hosts and hostesses everywhere. The preparation is time-consuming and the meal planning (and there are many meals) can be overwhelming. That is why I created, **Passover by Design**. I've scrutinized all the Passover-possible recipes from the previous four books and selected the best of the best that could be converted for Passover use. Each selected recipe has been reworked for this holiday and retested to insure its ease of preparation, its eye appeal, and, of course, its delicious results.

I've also included over 30 brand-new recipes. Many are exclusive dishes personally designed by **Moshe David**, of Fig and Palm, a rising new star on the kosher catering scene. Although his recipes are more intricate, I think seasoned chefs, looking for cutting-edge restaurant-style foods, will find them exciting. Collaborating with Moshe opened my eyes to some wonderful, healthy cooking techniques as well as some very creative new dishes I never dreamed could be used for Passover.

The word "seder" means "order." There's a reason and significance to everything that is found on the seder table and that takes place during the seder. Let your preparations reflect a similar "order." Plan your meals carefully so that you don't over-plan. Make your menus and shopping lists early so your meals make sense and you are not stressed. Holidays are a personal event and should reflect your family's traditions and that includes foods that have been around your table for generations. However, it is fun to introduce new foods to the old and to vary dishes, making menus that include both. I hope **Passover by Design** will become a valuable Passover tool for doing this.

With all the ingredient substitutions done for you, you will have more time to focus on what you love about preparing for Passover — making delicious foods that bring family and friends together in celebration of the holiday.

Susie Fishbein

On a technical note familiar to Jewish cooks of Ashkenaz tradition, **Passover by Design** includes some recipes that include *gebrokts*, a Yiddish word meaning "broken." This refers to using "broken" matzo or matzo meal mixed with liquid. Certain Chassidic traditions refrain from gebrokts during Passover, while other streams of Eastern European influence do "eat *gebrokts*." Each recipe is marked so you will know which are appropriate for your family.

Table of Contents

Preparing the Seder

The seder preparations should be made in time for the seder to begin as soon as the synagogue services are finished; it should not begin before nightfall, however. Matzo, bitter herbs, and several other items of symbolic significance are placed on the seder plate. Most people customarily follow the arrangement as shown below in setting this plate.

MATZO — Three whole matzos are placed one atop the other, separated by a cloth or napkin. Matzo must be eaten three times during the seder: by itself, with maror, and as the afikoman. Each time, the minimum portion of matzo for each person should have a volume equivalent to half an egg. Where many people are present, enough matzos should be available to enable each participant to receive a proper portion.

MAROR[1] and **CHAZERET**[2] — Bitter herbs are eaten twice during the seder, once by themselves and a second time with matzo. Each time a minimum portion, equal to the volume of half an egg, should be eaten. The Talmud lists several vegetables that qualify as maror, two of which are put on the seder plate in the places marked *chazeret* and *maror*. Most people use romaine lettuce (whole leaves or stalks) for chazeret, and horseradish (whole or grated) for maror, although either may be used for the mitzvah of eating maror later in the seder.

3 Matzos

CHAROSET[3] — The bitter herbs are dipped into charoset (a mixture of grated apples, nuts, other fruit, cinnamon and other spices, and red wine). The charoset has the appearance of mortar to symbolize the lot of the Hebrew slaves, whose lives were embittered by hard labor with brick and mortar.

Z'ROA[4] [roasted bone] and **BEITZAH**[5] [roasted egg] — On the eve of Passover in the Holy Temple in Jerusalem, two sacrifices were offered and their meat roasted and eaten at the seder feast. To commemorate these two sacrifices, we place a roasted bone (with some meat on it) and a roasted hard-boiled egg on the seder plate.

The egg, a symbol of mourning, is used in place of a second piece of meat as a reminder of our mourning at the destruction of the Temple.

KARPAS[6] — A vegetable (celery, parsley, boiled potato, carrot) other than bitter herbs completes the seder plate. It will be dipped into salt water and eaten. (The salt water is not put on the seder plate, but it, too, should be prepared beforehand, and placed near the seder plate.)

There are many variations on charoset. Everyone has their family tradition on how to make it. The recipe for Traditional Charoset comes from my family, and the Turkish Charoset is a nice alternative.

Traditional Charoset

PARVE ▪ MAKES 6 SERVINGS ▪ NON-GEBROKTS

When choosing your sweet wine, pick something thick, like Malaga or Concord. This way the mixture will remain thick and not watery even after the chopped apples and nuts have been refrigerated.

Using a mezzaluna or double-blade chopper in a bowl, chop the apples and walnuts. Add the wine and cinnamon. Mix well. Cover and refrigerate until ready to use.

2 Red Delicious apples, peeled and cored

2 Braeburn, Gala, or McIntosh apples, peeled and cored

1 cup chopped walnuts

¼-½ cup sweet red wine

1½ teaspoons ground cinnamon

Turkish Charoset

PARVE ▪ MAKES 6 SERVINGS ▪ NON-GEBROKTS

This Turkish charoset can be left chunkier or ground to a thick paste. Unlike most Yemenite and Syrian charoset recipes, this one does not contain kitniyot. Leftovers are nice spread on matzo or served with chicken.

In the bowl of a food processor fitted with a metal blade, chop the raisins, dates, figs, and apricots. Add the walnuts, apple, and orange zest. Pulse to a smooth paste. Drizzle in wine to reach desired consistency.

¼ cup raisins

½ cup pitted dates

½ cup dried figs

½ cup dried apricots

½ cup almonds or walnuts

1 medium McIntosh apple, peeled and cored

zest from ½ orange

sweet red wine

...And have a bowl doing it!

When my daughter Danielle was 4 years old, she came home from nursery singing a hilarious Passover song called "Mrs. Balabusta." It is an endless list of all the tasks that need to be done to prepare for the Passover seder including sweeping, dusting, shopping, mopping, polishing, waxing, changing over the kitchen, cooking, setting the table, etc. By the end of the breathless song, we laughed hysterically and everyone joked that we hoped Mrs. Balabusta was still breathing and able to attend her seder.

The truth is, preparations for the host/hostess of the holiday are huge. But, by the night of the seder, it doesn't have to fall on only one or two people. Everyone can help out, and here is a fun way for them to do it that will also break the ice if you have guests at your table. Fill a fishbowl with all the tasks of the evening written on pretty sheets of paper. Include things like serving the first course, clearing the main

course dishes, washing the wine glasses — all the chores that have to be tackled. Gather everyone around the table. Have each person fish out a paper and what they pick becomes their job for the evening. The fun really starts when people try, out of desire or necessity, to swap tasks. If a child gets "serve the soup," he or she will need to find an adult to switch with. Sometimes your guests may find it necessary to sweeten the deal to get someone to agree to the trade.

Think Inside the Box ...

Have you ever been the last one waiting on the line for the two times we get up to wash during the seder? Do you have elderly relatives who may find this getting up and down very difficult? How patiently have you waited as the bowl of charoset or vegetables for dipping gets passed around? If this speaks to you, then you will love this stylish entertaining idea.

As a matter of both décor and convenience I set my holiday table with an inviting bento box at each person's place. These beautiful boxes can be found inexpensively in Chinatown in New York City or at any large Asian supermarket. You can purchase them on the internet as well but they are pricier. They are typically used to serve sushi and are divided into compartments. In each compartment I placed one of the ceremonial seder items. There is a portion of charoset and a portion of maror, the divided section holds salt water and vegetables for dipping, and the remaining section has a sake flask filled with water and a tea towel for washing. Think of the ease your guests will experience as they reach right in front of them for the necessary seder item.

Don't be scared off by the bright colors and contemporary look. The trend in holiday table décor these days is modern or a mix of modern and traditional. Although your family's heirloom seder plate will certainly be the religious centerpiece of the table to be used by the leader of your seder, the bento boxes will provide comfort, convenience, and a cutting-edge addition to your Passover table.

Uncork a Conversation

We are required to drink a cup of wine at four specific points in each seder. This alludes to the four expressions of redemption mentioned in the Torah. To enhance the concept of redemption and freedom, we recline while drinking, have others pour the wine for us, and select red wines which are highly esteemed in Judaic tradition.

There are exceptional kosher for Passover wines available from all over the world in all sorts of varietals. This year, give this aspect of your seder even more personal meaning. Make your wine selections pointed and relevant so that the bottles of wine themselves enrich your seder.

My wine bottles will be personal conversation pieces this year. My niece spent time as an exchange student in Chile this year so I will select a red wine from Chile and have her talk a little about the Jewish community there. I will be sure to include a wine from the northern vineyards in Israel to remind my family of our last trip to Israel for my eldest daughter's bat-mitzvah, when we stayed up north. My husband visited Argentina on a UJC mission and can speak of the community there as we pour from a bottle of wine from Argentina. Even on the clever side, there is a wine called Ohra Kal, a lovely, sweet, red wine from a vineyard in the outskirts of Jerusalem. With a husband named Kal and another bat-mitzvah trip upcoming that will be starting in Jerusalem, I know that this one is sure to be a crowd-pleaser at my table.

Find ways to connect your wine selections with a theme, whether they are bottles from places that Jews have been exiled from earlier in history or bits of research you can do about how Jews are living today in four different countries.

A personal or online visit to a well-stocked kosher liquor supplier will yield you infinite choices. From Australia, France, Spain, California, Italy, New Zealand, Chile, Argentina, Russia, and, of course, Israel, there are worlds of wine waiting to be uncorked and discovered.

Going Green

This eco-friendly idea is easy on the eyes and on the pocketbook. Recycle your Passover food packaging and re-use it by turning it into a smashing tablescape. While seder tables tend to be formal, the rest of the holiday can be a time for casual elegance.

Both cute and relevant, Passover containers, boxes, and tins come in various shapes and sizes. Group them together and fill them with floral foam. Stick in blooms of any shape and color. You can even garnish with fruit, leaves, or really gild the lily with dried fruit on skewers. Scattering flower petals adds width to the arrangement and color to the table.

You can also use this idea to make one-sided flower arrangements for a buffet-style meal. By standing various heights of containers against the back wall, you can extend the life of leftover flowers from the seder centerpiece when there are not enough flowers still alive to make a 360° centerpiece. Creative and efficient!

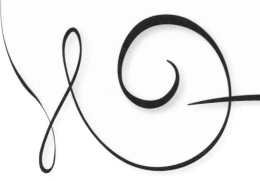

An Important Note About Kosher for Passover Ingredients

The number of Kosher for Passover products available to the consumer is tremendous and gets larger every year. The ingredients called for in this book were available kosher for Passover in the year that I was working on this project. Be aware that companies may add or pull items from their Passover lines.

Make sure you are using reliably certified Passover ingredients. It can be deceiving to see year-round products in identical packaging for this holiday. For example, confectioner's sugar is made with sugar and cornstarch. On Passover, confectioner's sugar is available but potato starch is substituted. You will find it certified. Vanilla is another example. Pure vanilla extract is produced with alcohol and on Passover you will find imitation vanilla.

There are also items that do not require Kosher for Passover certification on the label but still need a standard marking. The OU has a helpful website, www. oupassover.org, which is very useful on this and many other topics. If in doubt, consult your rabbinic authority.

You can always improvise to accommodate changes from year to year. If canned whole tomatoes are unavailable this year, but chopped ones are, substitute. If a recipe gives you directions how to make something that is now available ready to use, consider yourself fortunate and go for the added convenience.

APPETIZERS

Salmon Tataki	20
Meat and Potato Roll	22
Pistachio Chicken Skewers with Blackberry Sauce	24
Veal Loaf	26
Crispy Mushrooms	27
Steamed Sea Bass in Savoy Cabbage	28
Steamed Artichokes with Two Sauces	30
Teriyaki Chicken Satés	32
Moussaka	34
Sweet and Sour Meatballs	35
Tri-color Gefilte Fish	36
Portobello Stacks with Honey-Balsamic Ketchup	38
Antipasto Platter	40
Chicken Livers with Caramelized Onions and Red Wine	40

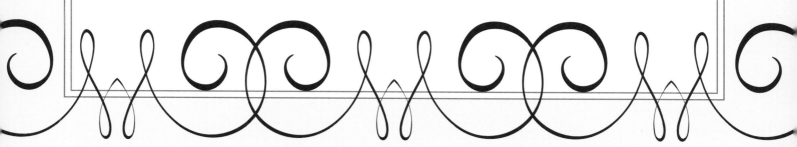

Salmon Tataki

PARVE ▪ MAKES 10 SERVINGS ▪ GEBROKTS

1 head cauliflower, trimmed into large florets

2 pound salmon fillet (6x9-inch rectangle), skin and pin bones removed

coarse sea salt

freshly ground black pepper

nonstick cooking spray

2 tablespoons vegetable oil

2 tablespoons matzo cake meal

1 tablespoon nondairy creamer

large daikon radish, peeled

fresh chives, for garnish

parsley sprigs, for garnish

You won't find gefilte fish on his table! Moshe David loves this adorable appetizer. The salmon is wrapped in a daikon radish collar and topped off with mashed cauliflower. It looks like a mini soufflé and is so elegant-looking. This recipe is not for beginners and I recommend using a real mandolin to cut the paper-thin slices of daikon. A hand-held model is too flimsy and can snap under the weight of the firm radish. If making a day in advance, keep the cauliflower separate. The salmon can be served at room temperature but the cauliflower needs to be reheated before topping off the fish.

Preheat oven to 350°F.

Place the cauliflower into a medium pot. Cover with water. Bring to a boil. Cook until the cauliflower is soft.

Meanwhile, place the salmon horizontally in front of you on the cutting board. Make a horizontal cut, cutting the thickness of the salmon in half, making 2 even large rectangles. Make sure the 2 pieces of salmon are even and thin. Trim any bumps and the ends to make sure they are straight. Season each with salt and pepper.

Cut 2 large aluminum foil rectangles, a few inches longer than the length of the salmon on both ends. Spray each foil with nonstick cooking spray. Place one salmon fillet on each foil. Starting with the longer side, using the foil to help, roll each fillet into a tube. Repeat with second fillet. Roll the foil, twisting the ends like a wrapped sucking candy.

Heat the oil in a large skillet. When the oil is hot, add the foil packets. Using tongs or a towel to protect your hands, gently rotate the rolls a ¼-turn as they start to sizzle, after about 1 minute. Once you have rotated each roll 4 times, exposing all 4 sides to the heat of the pan, remove from pan and place on a cookie sheet and into the oven for 15 minutes. Cool in the refrigerator for 15 minutes.

Drain the cauliflower. Place into a high-sided bowl. Season with salt and pepper. Using an immersion blender, purée the cauliflower. Add the cake meal and creamer. Purée until it reaches the consistency of mashed potatoes. Add more cake meal as necessary, ½ teaspoon at a time. Re-season with salt and pepper as necessary.

Remove the fish packets from the refrigerator. Slice the fish through the foil into 1½-inch pieces. Remove and discard foil. Lay each fish roll on a flat end on your work surface.

Using a mandolin, slice paper-thin lengthwise slices of daikon. Trim any wavy edges of the daikon slices. Wrap each salmon roll with a piece of daikon, wrapping the daikon like a collar around each fish roll. Trim the daikon if necessary. The fish should come up about halfway on the daikon collar. Spoon 3 tablespoons of the cauliflower on top of the fish, smoothing and leveling it off with a small metal spatula so it is even with the top of the daikon.

Move each salmon tataki to a plate. Garnish each plate with chives and a parsley leaf stuck into the center of each fish roll.

Meat and Potato Roll

MEAT ■ MAKES 8-10 SERVINGS ■ GEBROKTS

2 pounds ground beef

1 small onion, cut into ¼-inch dice

¾ cup matzo meal

2 tablespoons onion powder

1 tablespoon garlic powder

½ cup nondairy creamer

2 large eggs

1 teaspoon salt

¼ teaspoon coarse ground pepper

4 servings instant mashed potato flakes, prepared according to package directions

½ cup ketchup

3 tablespoons dark brown sugar

My mom and my Aunt Happy (yes, that is her name and yes, she always is), shared all of the holiday cooking for our family. This roll is a specialty of theirs. This dish has the comfort-food taste of meat loaf in a livelier presentation.

Preheat oven to 350°F.

Cover a jelly-roll pan with parchment paper. Prepare a second sheet of parchment paper. Set aside.

In a medium bowl, combine the beef, onion, matzo meal, onion powder, garlic powder, creamer, eggs, salt, and pepper. Use your hands to really combine.

Place your prepared jelly-roll pan lengthwise on your work surface. Place the meat mixture on the prepared pan. Pat to an even thickness, filling the pan widthwise and spread the mixture to an 11-inch length.

Prepare the potatoes according to package directions, adding more creamer, one tablespoon at a time, if they seem dry.

Place the potatoes across a shorter edge toward the bottom of the meat, but not at the very edge. Use the parchment paper to help you roll the meat into a log. Place the fresh sheet of parchment paper on the pan and place the meat roll onto it. Discard the original piece of parchment. Bake 1 hour, uncovered.

In a small bowl, mix ketchup and brown sugar. Brush over the meat roll and bake an additional 15 minutes.

Pistachio Chicken Skewers with Blackberry Sauce

MEAT ▪ MAKES 4 SERVINGS ▪ NON-GEBROKTS

CHICKEN SKEWERS:

4 boneless, skinless chicken breast halves

fine sea salt

freshly ground black pepper

1 cup white wine

1 cup shelled pistachio nuts, coarsely chopped

bamboo skewers, soaked in water for 15 minutes

BLACKBERRY SAUCE:

1 (15-ounce can) blackberries in heavy syrup (or substitute blueberries or sweet pitted cherries)

2 tablespoons sugar

1 teaspoon potato starch dissolved in 1 tablespoon water

The recipe calls for cutlets but the chicken tenders are the perfect size for these skewers. If your cutlets have tenders attached, you will need more cutlets. Just cut the tenders off and reserve the cutlets for another use. If the cutlets have had the tenders removed, follow the directions below.

Place chicken breasts into a plastic ziplock bag. Slightly flatten by pounding with the bottom of a saucepan. Cut each cutlet into 3 strips.

Season chicken strips with salt and pepper. Place them into a bowl. Add wine. Marinate for 1 hour.

Preheat oven to 350°F.

Remove chicken from the wine. Roll each strip in the chopped pistachios, pressing them into the chicken so they adhere. Thread the strips accordian-style onto the bamboo skewers. Bake on a cookie sheet for 13–15 minutes, turning once.

Prepare the sauce: Drain liquid from the blackberries, reserving liquid. Combine the blackberry liquid with the sugar and dissolved potato starch in a small saucepan over medium heat, whisking until smooth. Bring mixture to a boil; boil for 1 minute or until thickened and bubbly. Remove from heat. Stir in reserved blackberries.

Drizzle sauce over the chicken skewers and serve with remaining sauce on the side.

Veal Loaf

MEAT ▪ MAKES 14 SERVINGS ▪ GEBROKTS

VEAL LOAF:

nonstick cooking spray

3 tablespoons vegetable oil

2 stalks celery, cut into
   ¼-inch dice

2 large onions, cut into
   ¼-inch dice

2 cloves fresh garlic, coarsely
   chopped

1 (10-ounce) box white
   button mushrooms, cut into
   ½-inch pieces

¼ cup fresh parsley

1 (10-ounce) package frozen
   chopped spinach, thawed
   and squeezed dry

2 pounds ground veal

1 cup matzo meal

2 large eggs

¼ teaspoon freshly ground
   black pepper

GLAZE:

1 cup dark brown sugar

1 tablespoon red wine
   vinegar

5 tablespoons ketchup

This is a simple yet elegant first course. Anyone who knows me can tell you that I am freezer phobic, but even I must admit this one freezes beautifully. You can also double or triple the recipe with ease. I usually make a few of these at a time and freeze them.

If you don't have time to chop each of the vegetables individually, throw the celery, onions, garlic, mushrooms, parsley, and spinach together into the food processor and pulse a few times. This makes the preparation a snap.

Preheat oven to 375°F.

Lightly spray two small (9- by 5-inch) loaf pans with nonstick cooking spray.

Heat the oil in a large skillet over medium-high heat. Add the celery, onions, garlic, mushrooms, parsley, and spinach. Sauté until the vegetables are soft and fragrant. Remove from heat and cool for 5 minutes.

Add the veal, matzo meal, eggs, and pepper, mixing thoroughly. Divide the meat mixture in half and place into the prepared loaf pans.

Prepare the glaze: In a small saucepan over low heat, combine the brown sugar, vinegar, and ketchup. Stir until smooth. Pour the glaze over the veal loaves.

Bake uncovered for 1 hour. To serve, place a slice of veal loaf over pretty greens.

Crispy Mushrooms

PARVE ▪ MAKES 6 SERVINGS ▪ GEBROKTS

You can coat these mushrooms and keep them in the refrigerator for 3–4 days or even in the freezer for up to a month. You can cook them in the hot oil right from there. The temperature of the oil is vital. If it is too hot, the mushrooms will burn on contact but if it is not hot enough, they will just soak up the oil. Use a digital thermometer that measures over 350°F or a candy thermometer.

Fill a small pot with 3 inches of oil. Heat on medium until temperature reaches 350°F.

Meanwhile, whisk the eggs in a small bowl and set aside.

Mix the potato starch, salt, and pepper in a separate small bowl.

Pour the coating crumbs into a third bowl.

Working with a few mushrooms at a time, place them into the potato starch mixture. Toss until evenly coated, shaking off excess.

Place the mushrooms into the beaten eggs. Shake to coat evenly.

Place the mushrooms into the coating crumbs and toss to coat evenly. Set aside.

Continue until all the mushrooms have been coated.

Using a slotted spoon, lower the mushrooms, a few at a time, into the hot oil and cook for 2 minutes, until they are evenly cooked and golden-brown. Drain on paper towels. This may be done in batches.

Serve hot with warm marinara sauce.

vegetable oil

3 large eggs

1 cup potato starch

½ teaspoon fine sea salt

⅛ teaspoon freshly ground black pepper

1 cup Manischewitz Italian Herbed Coating Crumbs

1 large package button mushrooms, cleaned

jarred marinara sauce, warmed

Steamed Sea Bass in Savoy Cabbage

DAIRY OR PARVE ■ MAKES 6 SERVINGS ■ NON-GEBROKTS

1 head savoy cabbage, cored and separated into leaves

3 (6-ounce) sea bass fillets

fine sea salt

freshly ground black pepper

1 (10-ounce) package sliced lox

6 tablespoons white wine, divided

½ cup heavy cream or nondairy creamer

Looking for a light alternative to stuffed cabbage? This pretty Moshe David recipe looks like stuffed cabbage, but is a healthy, lovely fish dish that is mellow in flavor.

Bring a large pot of water to a boil. Drop the largest cabbage leaves into boiling water and blanch for 10 seconds, until they begin to wilt. Remove from the water.

Meanwhile, cut each sea bass fillet into 4 chunks. Season the sea bass with salt and pepper. Spread the lox out in pairs of overlapping slices on a piece of plastic wrap. Cover with another sheet of plastic wrap. Pound the lox with a meat pounder or the back of a knife to flatten and meld the pieces together. Wrap each sea bass chunk in a slice of the pounded lox. Depending on how wide the lox slices are, you may need to trim off excess lox to just cover the sea bass. Wrap each lox-covered sea bass chunk in a cabbage leaf, rolling it like a burrito or stuffed cabbage. Trim the cabbage if it is too long. Reserve these scraps.

Pour ¼-½ inch of water into a high-sided skillet or pot. Add 4 tablespoons wine. Bring to a gentle simmer. Add the sea bass rolls, making sure you are on a low enough heat that all you have are small bubbles. Cover the pot and steam the rolls for 15 minutes. Do this in batches if necessary. Reserve the fish broth.

In a small pot, heat remaining 2 tablespoons white wine. Add the cream and 1 cup of the fish broth. Add 2 tablespoons of the chopped dark green cabbage-leaf scraps.

Cut each cabbage roll in half on the diagonal. Lay one half on the other. Surround with the sauce.

Steamed Artichokes with Two Sauces

DAIRY OR PARVE ▪ MAKES 6 SERVINGS ▪ NON-GEBROKTS

1 lemon

6 large fresh whole artichokes, or 12 baby artichokes

fine sea salt

freshly ground black pepper

LEMON-CHIVE SAUCE:

½ cup (1 stick) butter or margarine, melted

1 tablespoon fresh lemon juice

1 teaspoon lemon zest

2 chives, finely chopped

BALSAMIC VINAIGRETTE:

½ cup extra-virgin olive oil

¼ cup balsamic vinegar

2 cloves fresh garlic, minced

1 tablespoon chopped fresh parsley

Artichokes may look strange, but they are fun to eat. The traditional way to eat steamed artichokes is to pull off one leaf at a time and scrape the tender meat from the lower edge of the leaf with your teeth. When all the leaves are off, your guests scoop out the fuzzy choke with a spoon and discard it. They are left with the "heart," the really delicious, flavorful center.

Artichokes are great by themselves but a dipping sauce adds extra flavor. When you are really short on time, bottled Italian dressing is a great accompaniment. If you have time, you may want to trim thorny tips off the outer leaves with kitchen shears.

Fill a large bowl with water and the juice of the lemon.

Slice the stem from each artichoke to form a flat base so the artichoke can stand upright on a plate. Discard the stem. While working with one artichoke, place the others in the bowl of lemon water to prevent them from discoloring.

Holding it on its side, cut off the top third of the artichoke. Pull back the outer leaves until they break off at the base. Stop when you get to the pale green layers. Repeat with remaining artichokes.

Place 2 inches of water in the bottom of a large pot and add 1 teaspoon salt. Stand the artichokes in the pot. Cover and place the pot over medium heat. Steam the artichokes until one of the leaves pulls off easily, about 25–35 minutes, depending on size. Drain and serve with choice of sauce. Remind your guests to discard the fuzzy choke before they enjoy the tender heart.

Lemon Chive Sauce: In a medium bowl, whisk the melted butter or margarine with the lemon juice, zest, and chives. Season with salt and black pepper.

Balsamic Vinaigrette: In a medium bowl, whisk the olive oil, vinegar, garlic, and parsley. Season with salt and black pepper.

Teriyaki Chicken Satés

MEAT ■ MAKES 6 SERVINGS ■ NON-GEBROKTS

TERIYAKI SAUCE:

- 4 teaspoons beef consommé powder
- 1 cup cola, not diet
- 1 tablespoon vegetable oil
- 1 clove fresh garlic, minced
- 1 (1-inch) piece fresh ginger, peeled and minced
- 2 tablespoons sugar
- 1 tablespoon honey
- ½ teaspoon potato starch, dissolved in 1 tablespoon water
- 1 tablespoon cooking sherry

CHICKEN SATÉS:

- bok choy or beet leaves
- 4-5 boneless, skinless chicken breast halves
- 24 shiitake mushroom caps, stems discarded
- fine sea salt
- freshly ground black pepper
- 4 tablespoons olive oil, divided
- 12 (6-inch) skewers, soaked in water for 15 minutes
- 3 cups bagged cole slaw mix
- 2 scallions, thinly sliced on the diagonal, for garnish

This is the dish that made me have to meet Moshe David. It was during Chol Hamoed Pesach last year that I called to check in on my friend and party planner, Renee Erreich. Renee was vacationing for the holiday at a resort in Orlando where Moshe was the caterer. As we spoke, she mentioned that they had had the most FABULOUS Chinese food for dinner the previous night. "Chinese food?!!" I exclaimed, knowing all soy sauce and the like are off-limits, making this a near-impossibility, and she said, "Yes, and I just had fluffy French toast for breakfast!" Once I regained my composure, I had her set up a meeting between me and this guy. My collaboration with Moshe for this book was eye-opening for me. This teriyaki sauce is one of his secrets and can be used in many dishes, so make a double batch.

Preheat oven to 400°F.

Cover a rimmed cookie sheet with parchment paper. Set aside.

Prepare the teriyaki sauce: In a medium pot dissolve the consommé powder in the cola. Simmer for 2 minutes. Remove from heat. In a medium pan, heat the oil. Add the garlic and ginger and sauté for 1 minute, until cooked through and starting to become golden. Add it to the cola. Add the sugar and honey. Whisk as it simmers for 1 minute. Whisk in the dissolved potato starch and simmer for 30 seconds–1 minute until thickened. Add the sherry. Remove from heat. Set aside.

Prepare the chicken satés: Fill a large bowl with cold water and ice cubes. Set aside. Bring a large pot of water to a boil. Drop the bok choy or beet leaves into the water and blanch for 5–8 seconds or until the leaves start to wilt and the color deepens. This is easy to do by placing the leaves into a strainer so they can all go in and come out at the same time. Remove the leaves and place them into the bowl of ice water to stop the cooking.

Season the chicken and the mushrooms with salt and pepper. Heat 2 tablespoons olive oil in a large skillet over medium heat. Sear the chicken for 2 minutes per side; it is okay if the cutlets are still pink, they will finish cooking in the oven. Cut the chicken widthwise into ½-inch-wide pieces, discarding uneven ends.

Open the blanched leaves and trim the stems to make rectangles. Roll each piece of chicken in a blanched leaf, trimming excess once chicken is completely wrapped.

Heat the remaining 2 tablespoons olive oil in the same skillet. Pan-sear the shiitake mushrooms for 1–2 minutes per side to soften them.

On 6-inch skewers, thread the chicken and mushrooms, folding the mushrooms as the skewer passes through them. You should start and end each skewer with chicken. Each skewer will have 3 wrapped chicken pieces and 2 mushroom caps. Use a knife to trim the edges so everything is the same size and lines up vertically.

Place the skewers onto the prepared cookie sheet. Remove 2 tablespoons of teriyaki sauce from the pot and use it to brush the skewered chicken and mushrooms. Bake for 6 minutes.

Toss the cole slaw mix in a medium bowl with ¼ cup of the teriyaki sauce. Pile ½ cup of the cole slaw mix in a mound in the center of each plate. Lay 2 skewers on the plate, criss-crossing over the cole slaw. Drizzle teriyaki sauce over each mound. Garnish with scallion.

Moussaka

MEAT ▪ MAKES 8 SERVINGS ▪ GEBROKTS

nonstick cooking spray

1 large eggplant (about 1½ pounds), peeled or unpeeled, cut into ½-inch round slices

fine sea salt

2 tablespoons olive oil

1 medium onion, chopped

1 pound ground beef

2 tablespoons tomato paste

3 tablespoons red wine

1 (15-ounce) can tomato sauce

2 tablespoons fresh chopped parsley

1 teaspoon dried oregano

¼ teaspoon ground cinnamon

½ teaspoon garlic powder

freshly ground black pepper

3 tablespoons margarine

1 tablespoon potato starch

2 cups nondairy creamer

3 large eggs, whisked

2 beefsteak tomatoes, evenly cut into ½-inch slices

¼ cup matzo meal

For Simchat Torah my family invades the home of our friends, Rina and Moshe Fuchs. The fun and friendship we share with them is enhanced by Rina's generous hospitality, especially at mealtime.

By dinner time on the last night of the holiday, just when my husband thought it was safe to take a snooze and that none of us could even look at food for at least a week, out came this moussaka. When he awoke, only 20 minutes later, and jokingly asked if he had missed a meal, we pointed to the empty moussaka dish. Well, you snooze, you lose. Some dishes can't be missed, especially this Passover rendition.

Preheat oven to 350°F.

Spray a 9- by 9-inch square baking pan with nonstick cooking spray. Set aside.

Place the eggplant slices on paper towel. Sprinkle with salt. Top with a paper towel. Place a pan or other weight on top. Leave for 20 minutes. This salting will draw out the bitterness from the eggplant and the salt will be drawn out with it.

Meanwhile, heat the olive oil in a large skillet. Add the chopped onion. Sauté for 4-5 minutes, until beginning to soften. Add the ground beef, breaking it up with a fork. Sauté for 15 minutes. Add the tomato paste, wine, tomato sauce, parsley, oregano, cinnamon, and garlic powder. Simmer for 15 minutes, until the mixture is almost dry. Season with salt and pepper.

Lay half the eggplant slices in the prepared pan. Pour the meat mixture over the eggplant. Top with remaining eggplant slices. Press down to compact.

In a small pot, over medium-low heat, melt the margarine. Add potato starch, whisking for 1 minute. Add the creamer, whisking until smooth. Simmer for 2 minutes, whisking constantly. Mix a small amount of the hot liquid into the eggs to temper them so they don't scramble. Add the egg mixture to the pot and bring to a low boil, whisking constantly. As soon as you see small bubbles, remove custard from heat.

Pour over the meat. Arrange the tomato slices over the top. Sprinkle with matzo meal.

Cover loosely with foil and bake 1 hour. Uncover and cook for 10 minutes longer until golden brown and bubbling around the edges.

Sweet and Sour Meatballs

MEAT ▪ MAKES 8 SERVINGS ▪ GEBROKTS

Place the ground beef into a mixing bowl. Add matzo meal, onion powder, and oregano. Add the egg. Toss the mixture with your hands until it is combined.

Empty the can of cranberry sauce and jar of marinara sauce into a medium pot. Place over medium heat and cook for 5 minutes, stirring often with a spoon.

Roll meat mixture into balls the size of large marbles, and carefully add them to the pot. Set the heat as low as possible. Cover the pot and cook for 40 minutes. Transfer to a serving bowl.

1 pound ground beef

¼ cup matzo meal

1 teaspoon onion powder

1 teaspoon dried oregano

1 large egg

1 (16-ounce) can of whole berry cranberry sauce

1 (26-ounce) jar of your favorite marinara sauce

Tri-color Gefilte Fish

PARVE ▪ MAKES 10-12 SERVINGS ▪ NON-GEBROKTS

nonstick cooking spray

2 (22-ounce) loaves plain gefilte fish, defrosted in wrapper

1 (22-ounce) loaf salmon gefilte fish, defrosted in wrapper

2 tablespoons fresh dill, chopped

1 lemon

6 cucumbers for horseradish wells, plus a long cucumber for optional top garnish

prepared red horseradish

mayonnaise

yellow pepper, seeded, chopped into tiny dice, for garnish

This easy spin on traditional gefilte fish has three different colored layers for a sophisticated look. It takes only 5 minutes to prepare. The recipe is based on a 9-inch springform pan with a removable bottom. If you are using a larger springform pan you may need to use 1-2 loaves per layer. Playing with the amounts won't affect the cooking method, but you may need to increase the cooking time by 10-15 minutes.

Preheat oven to 350°F.

Spray a 9-inch springform pan with nonstick cooking spray. Give it a heavy, even coat. Open each gefilte fish wrapper.

Place one plain loaf into a medium bowl. Add dill and juice from lemon. Mix thoroughly so the dill is dispersed evenly. Set aside.

Using a thin spatula, spread the remaining plain gefilte fish loaf into an even layer in the bottom of the springform pan. Top with an even layer of the salmon. On top of the salmon, spread an even layer of the lemon-dill fish mixture.

Cover the pan with foil. Bake for 1 hour. If the fish does not look set in the center, remove the foil and bake 5 minutes longer.

Let cool and refrigerate overnight. Can be made a few days in advance. As an optional garnish, slice a long unpeeled cucumber by hand or by mandoline into paper-thin slices. Lay the slices in concentric circles around the top of the fish.

Release the sides of the springform pan. To serve as individual servings, cut into wedges, like a pie. Trim any brown edges.

Cut the cucumbers into 2- to 3-inch pieces. Hollow out the centers. Mix a few tablespoons of prepared horseradish with a little mayonnaise to make a pretty pink sauce. Fill cucumber wells.

Serve a slice of fish on a piece of leafy lettuce with a cucumber well. You can decorate each plate with tiny squares of yellow pepper.

Portobello Stacks
with Honey-Balsamic Ketchup

PARVE ▪ MAKES 6-8 SERVINGS ▪ GEBROKTS

vegetable oil

4 very large portobello
   mushroom caps

1 cup matzo meal

¾ cup matzo farfel

2 teaspoons imitation
   mustard

½ teaspoon fine sea salt

¼ teaspoon freshly ground
   black pepper

3 large eggs

6-inch skewers

HONEY-BALSAMIC KETCHUP:

½ cup ketchup

2 tablespoons balsamic
   vinegar

1 teaspoon honey

½ teaspoon fine sea salt

¼ teaspoon freshly ground
   black pepper

¼ teaspoon parve chicken
   consommé powder

These crunchy mushrooms with their sweet and sour dipping sauce are a great way to start a meal.

Fill a medium pot halfway with oil. Heat over medium to 375–400°F, maintaining this temperature throughout the cooking process.

Scoop out and discard the gills from the bottom of each portobello cap. Peel the skin from each cap and discard. Slice each cap into 8-12 triangles, depending on size of mushroom. Set aside.

Place matzo meal, matzo farfel, mustard, salt, and pepper into a shallow container. Using your fingers, toss to mix.

Place eggs into a second shallow container and whisk lightly.

Dip each portobello triangle into the eggs and then into matzo-meal mixture, patting it to coat well.

When all the mushrooms are coated, carefully lower one into the hot oil (it should gently bubble but not burn), and cook to a golden brown. If the oil is not hot enough, the mushrooms will soak it up like a sponge; if it is too hot, the mushrooms will burn. Once the temperature is correct, fry the mushrooms in batches, 1–2 minutes per side, until golden-brown. Allow them to drain on paper towels.

Skewer 3-4 mushrooms triangles on each skewer.

Prepare the Honey-Balsamic Ketchup: In a small bowl, whisk ketchup, vinegar, honey, salt, pepper, and consommé powder.

Serve 2 skewers per person with a small bowl of the dip.

Antipasto Platter

MEAT ▪ MAKES 6-8 SERVINGS ▪ NON-GEBROKTS

2 boneless, skinless chicken breasts

Italian dressing, bottled

12 thin asparagus spears

10 ounces button mushrooms

olive oil

kosher or coarse sea salt

freshly ground black pepper

1 whole salami, cut into large cubes

2 roasted red bell peppers (can be jarred), sliced

1 (6.5-ounce) jar marinated artichoke hearts, drained

assorted olives

Antipasto is a sumptuous array of Italian finger foods. It is a great family-style first course.

Pour the Italian dressing over the chicken breasts. Marinate 15 minutes.

Preheat oven to 425°F. Place the asparagus and mushrooms on a baking sheet. Brush with olive oil, sprinkle with salt and pepper. Roast for 12–15 minutes. Remove from oven; set aside.

Turn oven to broil and broil the chicken cutlets for 5 minutes on each side or until no longer pink. This can be done on a grill as well. Cut the chicken into large cubes and set aside.

Arrange your platter: Select a sectioned dish or a large platter. Skewer the salami cubes with 6–8 inch thin wooden skewers. Do the same with the chicken cubes and the mushrooms. Place on the platter. In separate piles or sections, arrange the asparagus, roasted red peppers, artichoke hearts, and olives.

Chicken Livers
with Caramelized Onions and Red Wine

MEAT ▪ MAKES 4 SERVINGS ▪ NON-GEBROKTS

1¼ pounds kashered chicken livers

2 tablespoons vegetable oil

3 large onions, thinly sliced

¼ teaspoon freshly ground black pepper

½ cup red wine, port, Madeira, or sherry

1 large egg, hard-cooked and chopped

2 tablespoons chopped fresh parsley

Chicken livers must be kashered in a specific way. If your butcher does not sell kashered liver, here are directions for kashering raw liver:

Use a disposable broiler pan and a special dedicated knife. Poke holes in the pan so that blood will be able to drain freely from it. Set the broiler pan directly into a much deeper disposable roasting pan of the same width and length, so that the broiler pan is elevated (deeper disposable broiler pan should have some water in it), leaving room for the blood to drain into the lower pan. After trimming all visible fat from the livers with the dedicated knife and rinsing them under running cold water 3 times on each side, salt on each side in the pan with kosher (coarse) salt. Immediately place the livers onto the broiler pan and broil immediately under an open flame until the blood is cooked out, and the livers are completely edible on each side, turning with a special dedicated fork or tongs. Immediately after broiling, rinse livers again under running cold water 3 times on each side. Dispose of the pans.

Cut chicken livers into bite-size pieces. Set aside.

Heat the oil in a large skillet over medium heat. Add the onions and pepper. Cook, stirring frequently, for about 15 minutes or until the onions are well-browned. Add the wine and simmer for 5 minutes.

Remove from heat. Add the chopped chicken livers. Place in serving dish and top with the egg and parsley.

SOUPS

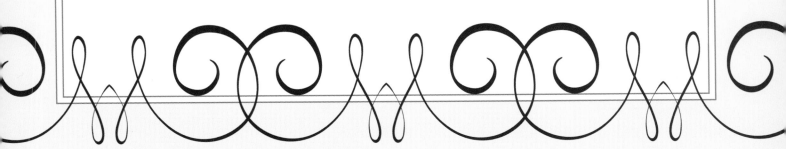

Creamy Peach Soup

DAIRY OR PARVE ▪ MAKES 6 SERVINGS ▪ NON-GEBROKTS

4 okra, thinly sliced to look like flowers

8 large white peaches, peeled, pitted, cut into chunks

juice and zest of 3 medium oranges

¾ cup jarred baby food carrots or puréed cooked carrots

½ cup heavy cream or nondairy creamer

2 teaspoons fine sea salt

1 tablespoon plus 1 teaspoon honey

2 teaspoons lemon juice

6 fresh chives, for garnish

You can use frozen peaches; they are usually peeled.

Place the sliced okra into a small pot of water. Bring to a simmer and cook for 3–4 minutes. Drain. Set aside for garnish.

Place the peaches, orange zest, orange juice, and carrots into the bowl of a food processor fitted with a metal blade. Pulse until smooth. Add the cream or creamer, salt, honey, and lemon juice. Pulse until creamy.

Serve the soup at room temperature or chilled, in bowls garnished with a few slices of okra and a fresh chive.

Carrot and Spinach Soup

MEAT OR PARVE ▪ MAKES 6-8 SERVINGS ▪ NON-GEBROKTS

2 tablespoons olive oil

2 cloves fresh garlic, chopped

1 small onion, chopped

4 cups chicken or vegetable stock

2 cups water

1 pound carrots, peeled and cut into 1-inch chunks

1 cinnamon stick

1 bay leaf

¼ teaspoon black pepper

½ teaspoon sea salt

1 tablespoon chopped fresh dill

1 sweet potato, peeled and cooked or microwaved for 7-8 minutes, or ½ cup canned sweet potatoes, drained

2 cups fresh baby spinach leaves

If the adages from childhood are correct, your eyesight and muscles will benefit in no time from this warm, delicious dish.

Heat the olive oil in a large pot. Add the garlic and onion. Cook for 5 minutes over low heat, making sure not to brown the onions, just soften them. Pour the stock and water into the pot. Add the carrots, cinnamon stick, bay leaf, black pepper, salt, and dill. Bring to a boil. Reduce heat. Simmer, covered, for 30 minutes.

Uncover; remove and discard the cinnamon stick and bay leaf. Add the sweet potato. With an immersion blender right in the pot, or in batches in a blender, purée the soup until smooth. Adjust salt and pepper. Add the spinach. Cook for 5 minutes, just until spinach is wilted.

Sweet and Sour Cabbage Soup

MEAT ▪ MAKES 8-10 SERVINGS ▪ NON-GEBROKTS

A hearty meal in a bowl. This soup is even better when allowed to sit a day or two before serving.

Heat the oil in a large pot over medium heat. Sear the flanken or short ribs on all sides, about 3–5 minutes per side, depending on thickness. Remove as they are done. Add the onions and garlic. Sauté for 3 minutes.

Return the meat to the pot. Add the cabbage, tomatoes, tomato sauce, beef stock, lemon juice, brown sugar, sauerkraut, and pepper. Bring to a boil. Stir. Reduce heat to low and cover. Simmer for 2 hours.

2 tablespoons olive oil

2 large strips flanken or beef short ribs, 2-2½ pounds total

2 onions, chopped

3 cloves fresh garlic, chopped

4 cups finely sliced green cabbage, about ½ of a small head of cabbage

1 (28-ounce) can whole tomatoes, finely chopped, with their juices

1 (8-ounce) can tomato sauce

8 cups beef stock (can be made from 8 teaspoons beef consommé powder and 8 cups water)

juice of 2 lemons

½ cup dark brown sugar

½ cup sauerkraut (from jar or can)

½ teaspoon freshly ground black pepper

Carrot-Coconut Vichyssoise

MEAT, DAIRY, OR PARVE ▪ MAKES 6-8 SERVINGS ▪ NON-GEBROKTS

CARROT-COCONUT VICHYSSOISE:

4 cups chicken or vegetable stock

2 medium Idaho or russet potatoes, peeled and diced

16 ounces baby carrots, or 2 cups sliced carrots

1 leek, sliced, white and pale green parts only

1 shallot, diced

dash ground white pepper

⅔ cup coconut milk

½ cup nondairy creamer or light cream

BALSAMIC GARNISH:

¼ cup balsamic vinegar

3 tablespoons pancake syrup

Coconut milk is a thick, creamy mixture of coconut meat and hot water. It is parve. It is sold in cans and is different from cream of coconut, which is very sweet and used mostly for drinks. The clear liquid inside a coconut is not coconut milk but rather coconut juice.

If you can't find the coconut milk for Passover and you are up to the task, you can make your own by cutting the meat of a small coconut into small chunks and puréeing them in a food processor fitted with a metal blade. Pour 2 cups of boiling water over and let it sit for ½ hour. Process again until smooth. Pour into a cheesecloth-lined bowl, squeezing the milk into a bowl. You need to use this within a few days or it will spoil.

Prepare the soup: Place the stock, potatoes, carrots, leek, and shallot into a medium soup pot. Bring to a boil, reduce heat, and simmer for 30 minutes, until vegetables are very tender.

Season with white pepper. Simmer for 5 minutes longer. Add the coconut milk. Remove from heat. Transfer to a blender and purée until smooth. You can also use an immersion blender right in the pot and purée for a full 3 minutes. Stir in the creamer or light cream.

Place the soup in the refrigerator and cool for at least 5 hours.

Prepare the garnish: Place the balsamic vinegar and syrup into a small pot. Bring to a boil, reduce heat, and simmer on low for 6–8 minutes, until reduced by half. Place in refrigerator; it will get thicker as it cools.

To serve, ladle the soup into bowls; with the tip of a spoon or a squirt bottle, add a swirl of the balsamic syrup to garnish each bowl.

Cream of Asparagus Soup

Nothing heralds Spring like asparagus. This creamy soup, like most soups, can be made in advance. If freezing, don't add the creamer until ready to heat and serve.

Thoroughly wash the asparagus and snap or cut off the tough ends. Cut off and reserve the tips. Chop the stalks into ½-inch pieces. Set aside.

In a soup pot, heat the oil over medium heat. Add the onion and leek; sauté for 5–7 minutes or until the leek starts to shine.

Add the chicken stock, potato, oregano, and nutmeg. Bring to a boil. Add the chopped asparagus stalks. Reduce the heat; cover and simmer for 35–40 minutes.

Pureé the soup in a food processor or blender. It can be done right in the pot with an immersion blender as well, but it will be a little thicker.

Return the soup to the pot and add the creamer, lemon juice, pepper, and sherry. Bring to a simmer. Add the asparagus tips; simmer for 10 minutes. Serve immediately.

- 1 pound asparagus
- 2 tablespoons vegetable oil
- 1 medium onion, chopped
- 1 leek, white and pale green parts only, thinly sliced
- 4 cups chicken stock
- 1 medium potato, peeled and diced
- ½ teaspoon dried oregano
- ⅛ teaspoon ground nutmeg
- ½ cup nondairy creamer
- 2 teaspoons lemon juice
- ¼ teaspoon freshly ground white pepper
- 2 tablespoons sherry or Marsala wine

Zucchini-Leek Soup with Ginger Cream

MEAT, DAIRY, OR PARVE ▪ MAKES 6 SERVINGS ▪ NON-GEBROKTS

3 tablespoons margarine or butter

3 medium zucchini, unpeeled, each halved lengthwise and cut into ¾-inch chunks

2 leeks, white and pale green part only, sliced

2 russet potatoes, peeled and coarsely chopped

2 cloves fresh garlic

2 sprigs fresh rosemary

2 bay leaves

7 cups chicken or vegetable stock

⅓ cup white wine

½ cup nondairy creamer or light cream

GINGER CREAM GARNISH:

¼ cup nondairy whipping cream or heavy cream

½ teaspoon ground ginger plus more for garnish

Melt the margarine or butter in a large pot over medium heat. Add the zucchini and leeks. Sauté until translucent but not brown, about 7–10 minutes. Add the potatoes, garlic, rosemary, and bay leaves. Sauté for 3 minutes, stirring occasionally.

Add the stock and wine. Simmer for 15 minutes or until the potatoes are fork-tender.

Remove and discard rosemary and bay leaves. Add the creamer or light cream. Using an immersion blender, purée the soup in the pot. This can also be done in batches in a food processor fitted with a metal blade or in a blender.

By hand with a whisk, or in a stand mixer, whip the cream until soft peaks form. Blend in ½ teaspoon ginger.

Pour the soup into bowls. Garnish with a dollop of ginger cream and a sprinkle of ground ginger.

Chicken Soup

MEAT ▪ MAKES 8 SERVINGS ▪ NON-GEBROKTS

1 chicken, cut in eighths, with skin on

4-6 chicken thighs or legs, with skin on

2 large parsnips, peeled

2 large carrots, peeled

2 stalks celery, cut into large pieces

1-2 large leeks, sliced in half and cleaned thoroughly

1 onion

1 turnip, peeled and quartered

1 bouquet garni of 10 parsley sprigs, 10 dill sprigs, 1 bay leaf, 10 peppercorns

1 tablespoon coarse sea salt or kosher salt

2 teaspoons freshly ground black pepper

A bouquet garni is a bundle of herbs tied together with kitchen string or placed into a cheesecloth bag. The flavors infuse into the dish, yet it is easily removable after cooking.

Place the chicken into a large pot and cover with cold water. Add an additional 4–5 inches of cold water. Bring to a boil. Using a small strainer, skim the fat and impurities from the top of the soup as they rise.

Add the parsnips, carrots, celery, leeks, onion, turnip, bouquet garni, salt, and pepper. Lower the heat and simmer, uncovered, for 1½–2 hours. Strain the foam and impurities off as needed. Season with salt and pepper to taste. Turn off the heat.

When soup has cooled to room temperature, pour it through a strainer. This will eliminate any chicken bones or stray skin. Return the vegetables and chicken pieces, discarding bones, to the pot. This also allows you to transfer to a smaller pot so that it will fit into your refrigerator.

Zucchini Soup

MEAT OR PARVE · MAKES 8 SERVINGS · NON-GEBROKTS

This soup can be served hot or cold.

In a large pot, heat oil over medium-high heat. Add the onions and garlic. Sauté until translucent, about 5–7 minutes.

Add the zucchini; sauté 3–5 minutes. Add the parsley, dill, and basil; sauté 2–3 minutes longer. Add the stock; bring to a boil. Simmer, covered, for 25 minutes.

Transfer soup in batches to the container of a blender; process until smooth. You may also use an immersion blender right in the pot. Season with salt and pepper to taste.

3 tablespoons vegetable oil

3 large onions, chopped

3 cloves fresh garlic, coarsely chopped

6-8 medium zucchini, with skin, ends trimmed, cut into chunks

1 tablespoon chopped fresh parsley

1 tablespoon fresh dill, chopped

1 tablespoon fresh basil, chopped (about 3-4 leaves)

7 cups chicken stock, or parve consommé powder dissolved in water

fine sea salt

freshly ground black pepper

Yukon Gold and Caramelized Leek Soup

MEAT OR PARVE · MAKES 8 SERVINGS · NON-GEBROKTS

Place the potatoes into a large pot. Cover with water by 2 inches. Add 1 teaspoon salt. Bring the water to a boil. When the potatoes are soft, remove from heat and drain.

In a second large pot, heat the olive oil over low heat. Add the leeks and sauté until caramelized, about 30 minutes. Add 4 cups of the stock and water. Season with salt and pepper. Add the potatoes. Using an immersion blender, purée the soup. Thin with stock as needed.

3 pounds Yukon Gold potatoes, peeled, cut into large chunks

fine sea salt

3 tablespoons olive oil

3 leeks, white and pale green parts only, cleaned and cut into 1-inch chunks

4 cups chicken or vegetable stock, plus 1 extra cup for thinning the soup

2 cups water

freshly ground black pepper

Cream of Sweet Potato Soup with Roasted Pecans

MEAT, DAIRY, OR PARVE ▪ MAKES 8 SERVINGS ▪ NON-GEBROKTS

ROASTED PECANS:

- 2 tablespoons margarine
- 1 cup chopped pecans
- 1 tablespoon pancake syrup

CREAM OF SWEET POTATO SOUP:

- 1 tablespoon extra-virgin olive oil
- 1 stalk celery, chopped
- 1 leek, white and pale green parts only, chopped
- 1 large shallot, chopped
- 1 medium onion, chopped
- 1½ pounds sweet potatoes (about 3 medium or 2 large), peeled and cut into small chunks
- 6 cups chicken stock or vegetable stock, divided
- ½ cup canned or frozen sliced carrots
- 1 teaspoon ground cinnamon
- pinch of gound nutmeg
- ¼ teaspoon fine sea salt
- 1 cup nondairy creamer or light cream

I dropped off a container of this soup at my neighbor Ed David's house and got the following message from him on my answering machine. "Hi, it's Ed, now you're just showing off." Nothing more to say except, try this recipe.

Prepare the pecans: In a small frying pan over medium-low heat melt the margarine. Add the pecans and syrup. Cook, stirring, for 4–5 minutes, until roasted. Transfer to a piece of parchment paper or foil. Pecans can be made two days in advance and kept in an airtight container.

Prepare the soup: In a large pot, heat the oil over medium-high heat. Sauté the celery, leek, shallot, and onion until soft and shiny, about 4–6 minutes. Add the sweet potatoes; sauté 2 minutes longer.

Add 4 cups of stock and bring to a boil.

Turn down to a simmer and cook, covered, for 20–25 minutes, until sweet potatoes are soft. Add the carrots, cinnamon, nutmeg, and salt. Heat through.

Transfer to a blender or food processor and process until smooth. You can also use an immersion blender right in the pot; purée for a full 3 minutes. Add remaining 2 cups stock and creamer or light cream. Purée 1 minute and heat through.

Ladle the soup into bowls. Serve with a small handful of roasted pecans in the center of each bowl.

Emerald Soup

MEAT OR PARVE ▪ MAKES 6-8 SERVINGS ▪ NON-GEBROKTS

1 tablespoon olive oil

2 leeks, white and light green parts only, thinly sliced

2 cloves fresh garlic, chopped

3 cups vegetable or chicken stock

1½ pounds fresh spinach (stems removed), coarsely chopped

1 cup loosely packed fresh dill, stems removed

½ teaspoon fine sea salt

¼ teaspoon freshly ground white pepper

1 cup nondairy creamer

cayenne pepper

The color of this healthful soup is just beautiful. It is a bright emerald green, hence the name. I like using precut fresh spinach from the bag. I grab a handful at a time, gather it together, and coarsely chop it with a knife. It takes no time at all to prepare.

In a large soup pot, heat the oil over medium-high heat. Sauté the leeks and garlic for 2–3 minutes, stirring frequently. Add the stock and bring to a boil.

Add the spinach, dill, salt, and white pepper. Cover and cook 5–6 minutes or until the spinach is very soft.

Transfer to a food processor or blender and process until smooth. You can also use an immersion blender in the pot. Return to the pot and bring to a gentle boil over medium heat for 5 minutes. Reduce the heat and add the creamer. Heat thoroughly, gently stirring. Do not bring to a boil.

After you ladle out each portion, sprinkle each bowl with the cayenne for flavor and color.

Parsnip Bisque

MEAT OR PARVE ▪ MAKES 8-10 SERVINGS ▪ NON-GEBROKTS

2 tablespoons olive oil

½ Spanish onion, diced

¾ celery stalk, diced

1-2 cloves fresh garlic, minced

6 medium parsnips, peeled and diced

2 Idaho potatoes, peeled and diced

8 cups chicken or vegetable stock

fine sea salt

freshly ground black pepper

fresh chives, for garnish

This comforting soup's velvety texture and beautiful creamy color are sure to warm your family on any cold winter night. If the soup gets too thick, which it usually does overnight in the refrigerator, thin with a little stock. Thanks for this recipe go to Damian Sansonetti, formerly the chef of Shallots NY.

In a large pot, heat the oil over medium heat. Add the onion and sauté about 6–7 minutes or until translucent. Add the celery and garlic; sauté 2 minutes longer.

Add the parsnips, potatoes, and chicken or vegetable stock. Bring to a boil. Cover and reduce heat to low; simmer about 30–35 minutes or until the vegetables are very tender.

Let cool. Transfer the soup in batches to a blender and purée. You can also use an immersion blender to purée the mixture until smooth. Season with salt and pepper.

For extra smoothness, you can strain the soup through a fine chinois. Garnish with fresh chopped chives in the center of each bowl, if desired.

Roasted Eggplant Soup

MEAT, DAIRY, OR PARVE ▪ MAKES 6 SERVINGS ▪ NON-GEBROKTS

Spices have a limited shelf life. Whole spices stay fresh for up to 2 years, peppercorns up to 5 years if kept in a cool, dark place. Ground spices need to be replaced every 6 months to a year. They don't spoil but become less potent. Crush dried spices in your hand. If there is no aroma or if you taste them and the flavor is not strong, replace your stock.

Preheat oven to 350°F.

Make diagonal score marks over cut side of the eggplant. Generously drizzle with olive oil and season with salt and pepper. Place cut-side-down on a baking sheet and roast for 25–35 minutes, until the flesh is tender.

Place 1 tablespoon of olive oil into a medium soup pot over medium heat. Add the carrot, celery, and onion. Turn the flame to low and slowly cook, uncovered, until tender, about 10–15 minutes. Add the garlic and thyme. Simmer for 2 minutes. Turn off the heat.

When the eggplants are roasted, scoop out the flesh and discard the skins. Add the eggplant flesh to the pot. Add the mint leaves and stock. Transfer to a blender or food processor and process until smooth. You can also use an immersion blender right in the pot, and purée until smooth. Return to heat and cook until heated through. Add the cream or creamer.

Prepare the garnish: Mix the red pepper, yellow pepper, and chives or parsley in a small bowl. Place a mound of this garnish in the center of your soup tureen or in a small pile in the center of the soup in each bowl.

2 medium eggplants, unpeeled, cut in half lengthwise

olive oil

fine sea salt

freshly ground black pepper

1 medium carrot, peeled and chopped

2 ribs celery, chopped

1 Spanish onion, chopped

2 cloves fresh garlic

2-3 sprigs fresh thyme, leaves picked off and minced, about ½ teaspoon

8-10 fresh mint leaves

4 cups chicken or vegetable stock

3 tablespoons nondairy creamer or heavy cream

GARNISH:

½ red bell pepper, seeded and cut into tiny dice

½ yellow bell pepper, seeded and cut into tiny dice

2 chives or 2 sprigs parsley, minced

Caramelized Parsnip-Carrot Soup

MEAT, DAIRY, OR PARVE ▪ MAKES 8 SERVINGS ▪ NON-GEBROKTS

2 tablespoons margarine or butter

½ medium onion, sliced

2 cloves fresh garlic, coarsely chopped

2 large shallots, sliced

3 parsnips, peeled and thinly sliced

12 ounces packaged grated carrots

2 tablespoons pancake syrup

1 tablespoon dark brown sugar

1 teaspoon dried thyme

zest and juice of 1 navel orange

½ teaspoon coarse sea salt or kosher salt

6 cups chicken or vegetable stock

PARSLEY-CREAM GARNISH:

1 cup nondairy whipping cream or dairy sour cream

1 cup fresh parsley, stems discarded, for garnish

Grated carrot is sold in bags in supermarkets in the salad section, usually near the coleslaw mix and bags of shredded purple cabbage. It is a convenience and cuts down on the cooking time. If you don't have them, use 12 ounces of baby carrots or thinly sliced carrots; the soup will just take a little longer to cook.

Melt the margarine or butter in a large pot over medium heat. Add the onion, garlic, shallots, parsnips, carrots, syrup, and brown sugar. Stir to combine.

Allow the vegetable mixture to cook and caramelize for 12–15 minutes, until shiny and browned. Stir to keep the grated carrots from burning. Lower the heat if necessary.

Add the thyme, orange zest and juice, salt, and stock. Cover the pot and cook for 10–15 minutes, until the vegetables are fork-tender.

Uncover the pot. With an immersion blender, purée the soup until completely smooth. This can also be done by transferring the soup to a blender in batches.

Prepare the garnish: Place the sour cream or nondairy whipping cream and the parsley into a quart-sized container. With the immersion blender, purée until the cream becomes light green in color. This can also be done in a food processor fitted with a metal blade or in batches in a blender.

Ladle soup into bowls. Garnish each bowl with a dollop of the parsley cream.

Broccoli and Almond Bisque

MEAT, DAIRY, OR PARVE ▪ MAKES 6 SERVINGS ▪ NON-GEBROKTS

1½ cups blanched almonds

1 tablespoon olive oil

2 small onions, chopped

2 heads broccoli, florets cut off and stalks coarsely chopped

2 potatoes, peeled and cut into ½-inch cubes

5 cups chicken or vegetable stock

1 teaspoon dried tarragon

1 teaspoon imitation Dijon mustard

1 cup nondairy creamer or light cream

fine sea salt

freshly ground black pepper

You don't have to be a vegetarian to appreciate this creamy, aromatic soup.

Place the almonds in the container of a food processor fitted with a metal blade. Process until finely ground but not pasty. Set aside.

Heat the oil in a large pot over medium heat. Add the onions. Sauté until translucent, 4–6 minutes. Add the broccoli, potatoes, stock, tarragon, and 1 cup of the ground almonds. Cover and simmer for 20–25 minutes, until broccoli is tender.

Transfer to a blender or food processor and process until smooth. You can also use an immersion blender right in the pot to purée until smooth. Add mustard and cream. Blend.

Season with salt and black pepper as needed.

Garnish each bowl of soup with a sprinkle of the ground almonds.

Wild Mushroom Velouté Soup

MEAT, DAIRY, OR PARVE ▪ MAKES 8 SERVINGS ▪ NON-GEBROKTS

A velouté is a thickened soup, similar to a bisque. It is quick-cooking and so simple to prepare. In some markets, the wild mushrooms are packaged together. You can just buy 18-20 ounces total of the assorted packages.

I love the covered crocks pictured here. I use them often for soups and stews but my favorite use is for serving individual portions of cholent on Shabbos.

Heat oil in medium pot over medium heat. Add the mushrooms and sauté until tender, about 4 minutes. Add the garlic and onion. Cook for 4–5 minutes. Sprinkle in the thyme. Add the margarine or butter and melt. Slowly sprinkle in the potato starch. The mixture will form a sticky paste called roux. Slowly add the stock and simmer; whisk well, scraping the bottom. Cook, uncovered, for 20 minutes to cook out the starchy taste.

Season with salt and pepper.

- 2 tablespoons olive oil
- 1 cup (about 4 ounces) sliced shiitake mushrooms, stems discarded
- 2 cups (6-7 ounces) sliced oyster mushrooms
- 2 cups (6-7 ounces) sliced crimini mushrooms
- 2 cloves fresh garlic, chopped
- 1 small onion, cut into ¼-inch dice
- ⅛ teaspoon dried thyme
- ½ cup (1 stick) margarine or butter
- ¼ cup potato starch
- 7 cups chicken or vegetable broth, warm
- ⅛ teaspoon fine sea salt
- ⅛ teaspoon freshly ground black pepper

Spinach Matzo Balls

MEAT OR PARVE ▪ MAKES 6 LARGE MATZO BALLS ▪ GEBROKTS

- 2 large eggs, plus 1 egg white
- 2 tablespoons olive oil
- 3 ounces fresh baby spinach leaves
- 1 cup matzo ball mix (usually both bags out of a box)

Due to the high water content of fresh spinach, these matzo balls may be a little harder to roll than the other two flavors. If this occurs, add some extra matzo ball mix or matzo meal, 1 teaspoon at a time, until the batter can be rolled into balls. You want to use as little extra as possible so that the matzo balls remain light and fluffy.

In a medium bowl whisk the eggs and the oil.

In the bowl of a food processor fitted with a metal blade, process the spinach until puréed. Squeeze the water out of the spinach.

Add the spinach purée into the egg mixture. Whisk to incorporate.

Sprinkle in 1 cup (2 bags) of the matzo ball mix. Stir in with a fork, mixing as little as possible. Don't overwork it. Chill in freezer for 20 minutes.

Meanwhile, bring a pot of water or chicken stock to a boil.

Wet your hands in a bowl of cold water. Using your hand, and manipulating as little as possible, scoop out a ping-pong-ball size of the mixture. Form into a ball with your fingertips, using no real pressure. Bring the water down to a simmer. Drop the balls into the water. Cover the pot and simmer for 20 minutes.

Tomato Matzo Balls

MEAT OR PARVE ▪ MAKES 6 LARGE MATZO BALLS ▪ GEBROKTS

- 2 large eggs, plus 1 egg white
- 2 tablespoons olive oil
- 3 tablespoons tomato paste
- ½-¾ cup matzo ball mix (usually 1-1½ bags out of a box)

What a thrill it was for me as these matzo balls and I proudly made our debut on the Today Show with Katie Couric!

In a medium bowl whisk the eggs and the oil. Add the tomato paste into the egg mixture. Whisk to incorporate fully.

Sprinkle in ½ cup (1 bag) of the matzo ball mix. Stir in with a fork, mixing as little as possible. Don't overwork it. Chill in refrigerator for 20 minutes.

Meanwhile, bring a pot of water or chicken stock to a boil.

Wet your hands in a bowl of cold water. Using your hand, and manipulating as little as possible, scoop out a ping-pong-ball size of the mixture, adding more matzo ball mix or matzo meal as needed. Form into a ball with your fingertips, using no real pressure. Bring the water down to a simmer. Drop the balls into the water. Cover the pot and simmer for 20 minutes.

Turmeric Matzo Balls

MEAT OR PARVE ▪ MAKES 6 LARGE MATZO BALLS ▪ GEBROKTS

In a medium bowl whisk the eggs and the oil.

Add the turmeric into the egg mixture. Whisk to incorporate to an even yellow color.

Sprinkle in ½ cup (1 bag) of the matzo ball mix. Stir in with a fork, mixing as little as possible. Don't overwork it. Chill in refrigerator for 20 minutes.

Meanwhile, bring a pot of water or chicken stock to a boil.

Wet your hands in a bowl of cold water. Using your hand, and manipulating as little as possible, scoop out a ping-pong-ball size of the mixture, adding more matzo ball mix or matzo meal as needed. Form into a ball with your fingertips, using no real pressure. Bring the water down to a simmer. Drop the balls into the water. Cover the pot and simmer for 20 minutes.

2 large eggs, plus 1 egg white

2 tablespoons vegetable oil

1 teaspoon ground turmeric

½-¾ cup matzo ball mix (usually 1-1½ bags out of a box)

Strawberry-Blueberry Swirl Soup

DAIRY • MAKES 4 SERVINGS • NON-GEBROKTS

STRAWBERRY SOUP:

2 cups fresh strawberries, quartered

1 cup vanilla yogurt

½ cup sour cream

1 teaspoon vanilla extract

3 tablespoons sugar

BLUEBERRY SOUP:

1 cup fresh blueberries

1 cup vanilla yogurt

½ cup sour cream

1 teaspoon vanilla extract

3 tablespoons sugar

Prepare the strawberry soup: Place the strawberries, yogurt, sour cream, vanilla, and sugar into the bowl of a food processor fitted with a metal blade or blender. Pulse for 1 minute until the mixture is smooth.

Pour the strawberry soup into a medium bowl or large measuring cup big enough to hold it. Set aside.

Prepare the blueberry soup: Place the blueberries into the food processor or blender. Pulse for 1 minute until smooth.

Place a small mesh strainer over a medium bowl. Using a silicone or rubber spatula, scoop out the blueberries and put them into the strainer. Press with the spatula to extract the juice from the blueberries. Discard skins.

Add the yogurt, sour cream, vanilla, and sugar to the strained blueberries. Whisk to combine.

To serve, take 2 teacups. Fill 1 cup with the strawberry soup and 1 cup with the blueberry soup. At the same time, pour them into a bowl so that they meet in the middle. With the tines of a fork, swirl the two soups together.

Mini-Meatball Soup

MEAT ▪ MAKES 6 SERVINGS ▪ GEBROKTS

Over medium heat, bring the stock to a boil in a large pot. Turn the heat down to a low simmer.

Place the ground beef into a medium bowl. Add the matzo meal, oregano, and garlic. Lightly mix, but don't over-mix or the meatballs will toughen.

Roll the meat mixture into mini meatballs, the size of large marbles. Carefully drop the meatballs into the barely simmering stock. Cook, covered, for 8 minutes.

Make a stack of the spinach leaves. Slice into thin ribbons. Repeat with the basil leaves. Add the sliced spinach and basil to the pot. Simmer for another 10 minutes, uncovered.

Season with salt and black pepper to taste. Ladle into bowls.

6 cups chicken stock
½ pound ground beef
⅛ cup seasoned matzo meal
¼ teaspoon dried oregano
2 cloves fresh garlic, minced
30 fresh baby spinach leaves
5 fresh basil leaves
fine sea salt
freshly ground black pepper

Creamy Tomato Soup

DAIRY OR PARVE ▪ MAKES 8 SERVINGS ▪ NON-GEBROKTS

3 tablespoons olive oil

½ large onion or 1 medium onion, chopped

1 shallot, thinly sliced

½ leek, white and pale green parts only, thinly sliced

2 (28-ounce) cans whole peeled Italian tomatoes

2 tablespoons butter or margarine

½ cup heavy cream or nondairy creamer

This very simple favorite takes no time to prepare. I'm usually a big fan of the immersion blender that purées soup right in the pot, but for this recipe you should purée the soup in a blender or food processor fitted with a metal blade. You will be rewarded with an incredibly smooth, creamy, family-pleasing treasure. The best tomatoes for this soup are the whole peeled ones, sometimes called Italian or plum tomatoes. The cans usually have basil in them even when not listed in the title. Check the ingredient list; the basil just adds to the flavor.

In a large soup pot, heat the oil over medium heat. Add the onion, shallot, and leek. Sauté for 5–7 minutes or until they soften. Add the tomatoes and simmer, covered, for 15–20 minutes.

Add the butter or margarine; after it melts, add the cream. Remove from heat.

Transfer in batches to a food processor or blender. Run the machine for a full 40–50 seconds on each batch. This soup can be made in advance, but if you are going to freeze it, don't add the butter and cream until just before serving.

SALADS

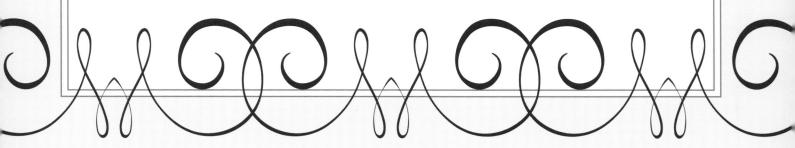

Julienne Salad

PARVE ▪ MAKES 6 SERVINGS ▪ NON-GEBROKTS

zest and juice from 1 orange

4 teaspoons imitation mustard

2 teaspoons honey

1 teaspoon apple cider vinegar

¼ teaspoon fine sea salt

¼ teaspoon freshly ground black pepper

2 large carrots, peeled, julienned

1 daikon radish (the size of a medium carrot), peeled, julienned

1 English hothouse cucumber, unpeeled, seeded, julienned

2 (11-ounce) cans mandarin oranges, drained

1 head Bibb lettuce, separated into individual leaves

Julienning is a method of food preparation that involves cutting the ingredients into long, thin strips. In this recipe they are long, thin, and almost spaghetti-like. This requires either incredible knife skills or a special peeler called a julienne peeler. Zyliss makes a good one. It looks like a vegetable peeler but it has teeth that slice long, thin strips of the vegetables.

In a small bowl whisk the orange zest, orange juice, mustard, honey, vinegar, salt, and pepper. Set aside.

Place the slices of carrot, daikon, and cucumber into a medium bowl. Toss with the dressing. Add the oranges.

Set one Bibb lettuce leaf on a plate. Using a fork, twirl the vegetables like spaghetti and form a bed in the lettuce leaf. Repeat with remaining salad.

Blackened Steak and Asparagus Salad

MEAT ▪ MAKES 6-8 SERVINGS ▪ NON-GEBROKTS

BLACKENING SPICE MIXTURE:

- 2 teaspoons onion powder
- 2 teaspoons garlic powder
- 1½ teaspoons cayenne pepper
- 1 teaspoon white pepper
- 1 teaspoon black pepper
- 1 teaspoon paprika
- 1 teaspoon dried thyme
- 1 teaspoon dried oregano
- 1 teaspoon dried basil

- 1 (1½ pounds) London broil or ½ filet split
- 2 tablespoons olive oil, divided
- 1 pound asparagus, trimmed

DRESSING:

- 6 tablespoons olive oil
- 2 tablespoons white wine or apple cider vinegar
- 2 tablespoons chopped fresh parsley
- 1 tablespoon fresh lemon juice
- 2 cloves fresh garlic, minced
- 1 teaspoon dried basil
- ¼ teaspoon crushed red pepper flakes
- ⅛ teaspoon dried oregano

- mesclun mix with radicchio, about 1 handful per person

The spice mixture is a Cajun spice mixture made from basic spices that most people have on hand, but when mixed in the proportions below it is a fiery delicacy. Mix up some extra and keep on hand to blacken fish or chicken. The dressing is best made a day in advance. In a time pinch, you can easily substitute store-bought Cajun spice mix and bottled Italian dressing for this salad. If you are making the steak a day in advance, don't slice it until you are ready to serve, and make sure you don't overcook it; a perfect medium-rare will hold up best in advance preparations.

In a small bowl or jar, combine onion powder, garlic powder, cayenne, white pepper, black pepper, paprika, thyme, oregano, and basil. Can be made in advance and stored in a covered container.

Generously rub one side of the steak with the blackening spice mixture. If you like your food very hot and spicy, rub the second side with the spice mixture as well.

Heat the oil in a large pan over medium heat. Add the steak, spice-side-down first (if spicing only one side), searing for 10 minutes per side. Remove from pan and allow to rest for 10 minutes. Slice into paper-thin slices. Add 1 tablespoon olive oil to pan. Add the asparagus to the pan and cook until bright green and fork-tender, about 7–8 minutes. Remove from heat.

Prepare the dressing: In a small bowl, whisk the olive oil, vinegar, parsley, lemon juice, garlic, basil, red pepper, and oregano.

Toss steak and asparagus with the mesclun and toss with dressing.

Citrusy Chicken Salad with Warm Olive Vinaigrette

MEAT ▪ MAKES 6 SERVINGS ▪ NON-GEBROKTS

4 boneless, skinless chicken breast halves, pounded slightly

fine sea salt

freshly ground black pepper

3 tablespoons olive oil, divided

1 head romaine lettuce, torn into bite-sized pieces

juice of 1 lemon

1 (11-ounce) can mandarin oranges, liquid reserved

1½ teaspoons lime juice

12 pimiento-stuffed green Spanish olives, drained and quartered

12 pitted black olives, drained and quartered

1 ruby-red grapefruit, peeled and segmented

2 limes, peeled and segmented

1 cup red grape tomatoes, halved

Whether it is a lime, lemon, grapefruit, or orange, for pristine citrus segments follow these directions: Cut a slice off the top and bottom of the fruit to expose the flesh and allow it to stand flat. Using a paring knife, cut off the skin and white pith, following the round contoured shape of the fruit and being careful not to cut too much of the flesh. Trim off any remaining pith. Hold the fruit over a bowl to catch any juices. With the paring knife, cut on either side of each membrane to release a citrus segment. Let them fall into the bowl as you make your way around the fruit. You can squeeze what is left of the fruit for the juice.

Season chicken breasts with salt and pepper.

Heat 2 tablespoons olive oil in a medium skillet over medium heat. Add chicken and sear for 5–6 minutes. Turn the chicken over and cook on the other side for 5–6 minutes or until cooked through and no longer pink. Remove from the pan.

Meanwhile, place the romaine on a platter or in a salad bowl.

In a small bowl, whisk the lemon juice, liquid from the can of mandarin oranges, and the lime juice.

With the skillet still on the stove and the heat at medium, add 2 tablespoons of citrus juice, the remaining tablespoon of olive oil, and olives to the pan. Sauté until just heated through, about 45 seconds. Toss the olives and any pan juices with the greens.

Slice the chicken on the diagonal into thin slices. Add to the salad.

Add mandarin oranges, grapefruit segments, lime segments, and tomatoes. Toss with any remaining citrus juices. Serve warm or at room temperature.

Orange-Endive Salad with Warm Tomato Vinaigrette

PARVE ▪ MAKES 6 SERVINGS ▪ NON-GEBROKTS

1 teaspoon olive oil

1 large tomato, seeded and cut into small dice

½ teaspoon fine sea salt

½ teaspoon freshly ground black pepper

¼ cup orange juice

⅛ cup olive oil

1 large Belgian endive, thinly sliced

5 ounces mesclun greens with frisée

2 (11-ounce) cans mandarin oranges, drained

1 medium red onion, cut in half, thinly sliced

To shape salad greens into nice restaurant-style mounds, lightly dress the greens, pack into a plastic pint container, invert onto a plate and lift away the container.

Prepare the vinaigrette: Heat a small sauté pan over medium heat. Add the teaspoon of olive oil. Add the diced tomato and season with salt and pepper. Sauté for 3 minutes.

Add orange juice. Simmer 2 minutes longer to reduce by half. Whisk in olive oil. Remove from heat. Season with more salt and pepper if needed.

In a large bowl toss the endive, mesclun, oranges, and red onion. Dress with vinaigrette.

Health Salad

PARVE ▪ MAKES 10-12 SERVINGS ▪ NON-GEBROKTS

SALAD:

4 carrots, peeled and sliced

2 cucumbers, peeled and sliced

1 red bell pepper, seeded and thinly sliced

1 green bell pepper, seeded and thinly sliced

1 head green cabbage, coarsely shredded

DRESSING:

½ cup vegetable oil

½ cup white vinegar

½ cup honey

1 tablespoon fine sea salt

This salad has found its way onto the tables of many delis and restaurants. Simple to make in advance, the dish pairs nicely with barbecue.

In a large bowl, combine the carrots, cucumbers, red bell pepper, green bell pepper, and cabbage.

Prepare the dressing: In a jar or cruet, mix oil, vinegar, honey, and salt. Shake well to mix. Pour over salad. Allow to marinate for at least ½-hour. Mix well before serving.

Mango-Tuna Salad with Goat Cheese

DAIRY • MAKES 6 SERVINGS • NON-GEBROKTS

You could use store-bought sun-dried tomatoes, either drained if they were in oil or reconstituted if they were dry. But try these homemade ones once; you won't go back. Using a low, dry heat adds intense flavor to tomatoes. They laze away as the moisture is slowly drawn out and sugars caramelize.

Prepare the dressing: In a small pot, combine mango, vinegar, orange juice, vanilla sugar, and salt. Bring to a boil and then simmer 3 minutes. Purée with an immersion blender right in the pot or transfer to a food processor and purée. Whisk in olive oil. Set aside. Can be made 2 days in advance and stored in refrigerator. Bring to room temperature to serve.

Prepare the honeyed walnuts: Heat oil in a small skillet over medium heat. Add walnuts and honey. Sauté for 3 minutes, making sure they don't burn. Remove from pan and place in a single layer on a piece of parchment or foil. Allow to cool. Keep in an airtight container for up to 1 week.

Prepare the salad: Toss mesclun with olive oil and balsamic. Arrange on a plate or platter.

Lay 3–4 tomato strips on the plate. Toss in honeyed walnuts.

Slice goat cheese into rounds and place in center of salad. Using a small ice-cream scoop, place tuna scoops between the goat cheese slices.

Drizzle with mango dressing.

DRESSING:
- 2 ripe mangoes, peeled, pitted, and cut into cubes
- ¼ cup white wine vinegar or apple cider vinegar
- ¼ cup orange juice (can use store-bought but not from concentrate)
- 2 tablespoons vanilla sugar
- 1 teaspoon fine sea salt
- 2 tablespoons extra-virgin olive oil

HONEYED WALNUTS:
- 1 tablespoon vegetable oil
- 1 cup walnut halves
- 2 tablespoons honey

SALAD:
- 5 ounces mesclun mix
- 2 tablespoons olive oil
- 1 tablespoon balsamic vinegar
- 6 sun-dried tomatoes, sliced into strips (see recipe on page 166)
- 4 ounces goat cheese
- ½ pound store-bought tuna fish salad, or 1 can tuna fish prepared to your liking

Shredded Greens
in a Lemon Zest Vinaigrette

PARVE ▪ MAKES 4 SERVINGS ▪ NON-GEBROKTS

¼ cup balsamic vinegar

1 tablespoon imitation
Dijon mustard

¼ teaspoon fine salt

⅛ teaspoon freshly ground
black pepper

2 teaspoons finely grated
lemon zest (yellow only,
not the white pith)

pinch of sugar

¾ cup olive oil

1 head Belgian endive,
thinly sliced

2 cups radicchio (about
¾ head), thinly sliced

1 cup fresh baby spinach
leaves

1 cup grape tomatoes

This is a light and fresh-tasting spring salad. The zest gives the dish a bright, enticing flavor. Use a microplane for ease.

In a jar or cruet whisk or shake together vinegar, mustard, salt, pepper, lemon zest, and sugar. Slowly add olive oil. Whisk or shake until combined.

In a large mixing bowl combine endive, radicchio, and spinach. Drizzle with the dressing and toss to combine. Add the tomatoes.

Hearts of Palm Salad

PARVE ▪ MAKES 10-12 SERVINGS ▪ NON-GEBROKTS

5-6 ripe Haas avocados,
peeled, pitted, and diced

1 (17-ounce) can hearts of
palm, drained and sliced

½ cup red onion, chopped

2 cups grape or cherry
tomatoes, halved

1 heaping tablespoon
mayonnaise

fine sea salt

freshly ground black pepper

juice from ½ lemon

This salad also serves double duty as a great side dish.

Lemon juice never seems to do the trick of keeping cut avocado halves green. The key is keeping light and air away. If preparing the avocados in advance, lightly spray the exposed flesh with cooking spray. Wrap in foil and refrigerate until ready to use.

In a large bowl combine avocado, hearts of palm, onion, and tomatoes. Toss with mayonnaise. Season with salt, pepper, and lemon juice.

Chicken Salad with Cherry Balsamic Vinaigrette

MEAT ▪ MAKES 4-6 SERVINGS ▪ NON-GEBROKTS

The balsamic and cherries make for deep, wonderful flavors that complement chicken perfectly. Who needs a main dish with this salad?

Preheat oven to 350°F.

Cover a jelly roll pan with parchment paper. Set aside.

In a small bowl, whisk the brown sugar, 2 tablespoons of the reserved cherry juice, and olive oil. Season with salt and pepper. Add the walnuts, toss to coat. Marinate for 30 minutes. Drain the walnuts and spread in a single layer on prepared pan. Bake 8–10 minutes until glazed and golden. Set aside on parchment paper or foil. Can be made in advance and kept in an airtight container for up to 3 days.

In a tall container (to prevent splattering,) with an immersion blender, emulsify the balsamic, olive oil, cherries, salt, pepper, and mustard. This can also be done in a food processor.

Season both sides of each chicken breast with salt and pepper. Place the tablespoon of olive oil into a skillet over medium-high heat. Add the chicken and sear 5–6 minutes per side until golden brown on both sides. Remove from skillet and cut into dice.

Toss the dressing with the mesclun leaves. Add candied walnuts and chicken cubes; sprinkle with dried cranberries. Drizzle with extra dressing.

CANDIED WALNUTS:

- 2 tablespoons dark brown sugar
- juice from 1 (8-ounce) can sweet dark pitted cherries; reserve cherries
- 1 teaspoon extra-virgin olive oil
- fine sea salt
- freshly ground black pepper
- 4 ounces walnut halves

DRESSING:

- 2 tablespoons balsamic vinegar
- 4 tablespoons extra-virgin olive oil
- reserved, drained cherries from above
- ¼ teaspoon fine sea salt
- ¼ teaspoon freshly ground black pepper
- ½ teaspoon imitation mustard

CHICKEN:

- 4 boneless, skinless chicken breast halves, tenders removed
- fine sea salt
- freshly ground black pepper
- 1 tablespoon extra-virgin olive oil

- 5 ounces mesclun mix
- 1 cup dried cranberries

Mexican Turkey and Portobello Salad

MEAT ▪ MAKES 4 SERVINGS ▪ NON-GEBROKTS

4 portobello mushrooms

¼ cup balsamic vinegar

¼ cup olive oil

2 cloves fresh garlic, minced

¼ teaspoon fine sea salt

¼ teaspoon freshly ground black pepper

½ pound cooked Mexican style turkey breast, such as Hod brand, cut into cubes

4 ounces mesclun lettuce

5-6 chives, chopped

DRESSING:

1 tablespoon balsamic vinegar

1 shallot, sliced

1 clove fresh garlic, chopped

½ cup vegetable oil

3 tablespoons water

2 teaspoons imitation Dijon mustard

Preheat oven to 375°F.

Peel the skin from the cap of each portobello. Snap off and discard each stem. Using your hand to support the mushroom, use a spoon to scoop out as much of the gills as possible. Discard the gills. Place the mushrooms into a baking dish. Pour the balsamic, olive oil, and garlic into small bowl. Whisk together. Season with salt and pepper. Pour over the mushrooms.

Roast the mushrooms in the oven for 10 minutes, basting halfway through the cooking time. Remove from oven and cool for 5 minutes. Slice the mushrooms and mix with the turkey cubes.

Using an immersion blender in a tall container (to reduce splattering) or in the bowl of a food processor fitted with a metal blade, combine the balsamic, shallot, garlic, oil, water, and Dijon mustard. Pulse until emulsified.

Dress the lettuce. Mix in the turkey and mushrooms. Garnish with chives.

Warm Mushroom-Potato Salad

PARVE ▪ MAKES 6-8 SERVINGS ▪ NON-GEBROKTS

Certain foods remind us of certain people. Potato salads will always be a small reminder of my friend Lisa Goldenberg Altman, an extraordinary woman, who passed away at far too early an age. In addition to being a wonderful wife, mother, and lawyer, she was passionate about many things, including cooking. She had created dozens of versions of potato salad, which were in her recipe box. This one is a winning combination of some of those.

Place the potatoes into a medium pot. Cover with water. Bring to a boil over medium heat and cook for about 20 minutes or until the potatoes are tender when pierced with a fork. Drain and return to the pot.

Meanwhile, heat the oil in a medium skillet over medium heat. Add the mushrooms, scallions, shallot, thyme, sage, oregano, and basil. Sauté for 4–5 minutes, until the shallots and mushrooms are softened.

Add the mushroom mixture to the drained potatoes.

In a small bowl mix the minced garlic, salt, pepper, mayonnaise, vinegar, and parsley. Add to the pot and toss to coat the potatoes.

Serve warm or at room temperature.

2 pounds baby red potatoes, halved

2 tablespoons olive oil

6 ounces shiitake mushroom caps, cut into ½-inch dice

3 scallions, thinly sliced, white and pale green parts only

1 shallot, thinly sliced

⅛ teaspoon dried thyme

⅛ teaspoon dried sage

⅛ teaspoon dried oregano

⅛ teaspoon dried basil

2 cloves fresh garlic, minced

1 teaspoon fine sea salt

1 teaspoon freshly ground black pepper

⅓ cup mayonnaise

2 tablespoons apple-cider vinegar

¼ cup chopped fresh parsley

Smoked Turkey-Mango Salad

MEAT ▪ MAKES 6 SERVINGS ▪ NON-GEBROKTS

16 ounces smoked processed turkey, 1-inch thick chunk, not sliced

½ ripe mango, peeled and cut into ½-inch cubes

DRESSING:

juice of 1 lime

3 tablespoons mayonnaise

4 tablespoons apricot preserves

¼ teaspoon fine sea salt

¼ teaspoon freshly ground black pepper

½ cup roasted cashews, chopped

1 tablespoon fresh minced cilantro leaves

1 scallion, thinly sliced on the diagonal

⅔ cup baby arugula leaves

GARNISH:

2-3 fresh plums, halved, pitted and thinly sliced

4-5 fresh or canned apricots, halved, pitted and thinly sliced

6 scallion brushes

My family loves this Moshe David salad. I make it all year-round and it couldn't be easier. Sometimes I skip the garnish and just spoon it into Bibb or Boston lettuce cups.

Cut the turkey into ½-inch lengthwise slices. Stack the slices and cut into ½-inch cubes. Place into large mixing bowl. Add the mango.

Dressing: Place the lime juice, mayonnaise, and apricot preserves into a quart-sized container or bowl. Using a whisk or immersion blender, mix to form a smooth dressing.

Toss the turkey and mango with the dressing. Season with salt and pepper. Add the cashews, cilantro, and scallion. Toss to combine. Mix in the arugula leaves.

Garnish: Arrange 6 plum and 6 apricot slices in an alternating overlapping design on each plate. Place a mound of turkey salad in the center of each plate. Garnish with a scallion brush.

Roasted Beet Salad

DAIRY OR PARVE ▪ MAKES 8 SERVINGS ▪ NON-GEBROKTS

2 medium/large red beets, scrubbed but not peeled

2 medium/large golden beets, scrubbed but not peeled

olive oil

coarse sea salt or kosher salt

dried thyme

1 tablespoon honey

2 teaspoons imitation Dijon mustard

3 tablespoons orange juice

3 tablespoons olive oil

1 tablespoon balsamic or apple cider vinegar

2 ounce frisée lettuce

3 ounces red leaf lettuce

½ cup chopped walnuts

3 ounces blue or gorgonzola cheese, optional for dairy meals

Not one person in my family likes beets. Not one person left a drop of this salad over when I served it and it was requested the very next night! The roasted beets become almost like beet chips. They are incredible. The procedure can be done with taro root or other root vegetables as well. One of the unique aspects to this recipe is not needing to peel the beets.

Cutting the beets on newspaper keeps the juice from dying your kitchen pink, and gloves keep it off your hands. If you can't find golden beets, just double the amount of red beets.

Preheat oven to 450°F.

Line 2 cookie sheets with parchment paper. Slice off the top and bottom of each beet. Slice into rounds as thin as possible, ¼-inch thick or less. Drizzle each beet slice with olive oil, brushing it to evenly coat. Sprinkle with salt and thyme. Place on prepared baking sheet. Roast 18–22 minutes, until the beets are soft and slightly shrunken. Smaller or thinner beets will need to come out of the oven earlier so they don't burn. Set aside. Keep the colors separate as they will bleed.

Using an immersion blender or a whisk, combine the honey, mustard, orange juice, olive oil, and vinegar. Blend or whisk until emulsified. Season with salt and pepper.

Place the frisée and red-leaf lettuce leaves into a bowl and lightly dress, tossing to combine, reserving 6 teaspoons of the dressing.

Arrange the roasted beet slices, in alternating colors in a single layer on each plate. Drizzle a scant teaspoon of the dressing over the beets. Place a tall mound of the greens into the center of each plate, allowing the beets to peek out. Sprinkle with walnuts evenly over each plate. If using cheese, crumble over each mound of lettuce.

Purple Cabbage Salad

PARVE ▪ MAKES 8-10 SERVINGS ▪ NON-GEBROKTS

SALAD:

16 ounces shredded purple cabbage

⅓ cup chopped scallions

⅓ cup pine nuts

3 carrots, julienned, or 1 (8-ounce) bag shredded carrots

1 (11-ounce) can mandarin oranges, reserving liquid

1-2 handfuls dried cranberries (can be the sweetened kind)

DRESSING:

4 tablespoons brown sugar

½ teaspoon freshly ground black pepper

¼ teaspoon fine sea salt

4 tablespoons red wine vinegar

1 tablespoon reserved mandarin orange liquid

½ cup vegetable oil

1 teaspoon parve chicken consommé powder

½ teaspoon garlic powder

This salad also makes a wonderful side dish. It is a beautiful combination of colors and textures. Many men tell me they don't like fruit on their salad, but for some reason this salad is an exception to that rule. Thanks to my friend Beth Eidman for this treasure.

Place the cabbage, scallions, pine nuts, carrots, oranges, and cranberries into a large ziplock bag. Set aside.

In a jar or cruet, mix the brown sugar, pepper, salt, vinegar, reserved liquid from the oranges, oil, consommé powder, and garlic powder. Close and shake until thoroughly mixed.

Pour over the salad. Refrigerate to let the flavors mix for at least 1 hour. Can prepare early in the day.

Mediterranean Fatoush Salad

PARVE ▪ MAKES 6 SERVINGS ▪ GEBROKTS

This salad is so simple and refreshing. The spiced matzo chips can be made a few days in advance and stored in a ziplock bag. I always make some extra to serve with soup or dips at another meal.

Prepare the matzo chips below.

Slice the cucumbers in half lengthwise. With a spoon, scoop out and discard the pulp. Chop into ½-inch pieces. Place into a large salad bowl.

Thinly slice the endive and place into the bowl. Lay the mint leaves in a pile and tear them; they will bruise if you cut them with a knife. Add to the bowl. Toss in the parsley, tomatoes, and arugula. Mix in the lemon juice, olive oil, and garlic. Season with salt and pepper, tossing to combine. Allow to marinate for a few minutes.

Stand 2 matzo chips in each salad.

Spiced matzo chips (see below)

1 (8-10 inch) English cucumber, peeled

3-4 heads Belgian endive, separated into leaves

⅛ cup fresh mint leaves (discard stems)

¼ cup flat-leaf Italian parsley leaves (discard stems)

1 cup small grape or cherry tomatoes, quartered

1 cup arugula

juice of 1 lemon

4 tablespoons extra-virgin olive oil

1 clove fresh garlic, minced

pinch of coarse sea salt or kosher salt

½ teaspoon freshly ground black pepper

Spiced Matzo Chips

PARVE ▪ MAKES 6 SERVINGS ▪ GEBROKTS

Preheat oven to 350°F.

Brush matzo boards with olive oil. Sprinkle with shwarma spice, parsley, turmeric, and garlic. Place on baking sheet and bake for 8 minutes. Break into shards.

4 whole matzo boards

olive oil

1 teaspoon shwarma spice

½ teaspoon dried parsley

½ teaspoon ground turmeric

½ teaspoon garlic powder

Grilled Beef and Radish Salad

MEAT ▪ MAKES 6 SERVINGS ▪ NON-GEBROKTS

1½ pounds London broil or
    filet split

fine sea salt

freshly ground black pepper

2 tablespoons olive oil

1 daikon radish (look for a
   small one, about the size
   of a parsnip), peeled

3 red radishes, thinly sliced

2 cups alfalfa sprouts

1 cup baby arugula

½ cup chopped fresh parsley

¼ cup chopped fresh cilantro

¼ cup extra-virgin olive oil

2 tablespoons lime juice

Radish is a root vegetable. Both the bulb and the leaves are edible, though I call for just the bulbs in this recipe. The leaves tend to be on the bitter side. Daikon radish is shaped like a large carrot but is white in color. It can be eaten raw, although it is often used in Japanese stir-fry dishes. I love its crunch in this salad. Be sure to wash it well and peel just a thin layer from the outside. Stick to alfalfa sprouts as many other sprouts are bean sprouts, making them legumes and not suitable for Passover; or if in doubt, leave them out.

Thinly slice the steak on the bias. Season the slices with salt and pepper.

Heat the 2 tablespoons olive oil in a large skillet over medium heat. Add the meat and sear for 2–3 minutes per side, using tongs to turn the pieces. Remove the steak slices as they are done and set the meat aside.

Cut the daikon in half lengthwise. Thinly slice into half-moons.

Place the daikon and red radish into a large mixing bowl. Add the sprouts, arugula, parsley, and cilantro. Toss in ¼ cup of extra-virgin olive oil and lime juice.

Arrange the salad on a plate or platter and lay the beef slices on top. Serve warm or at room temperature.

New Millennium Waldorf Salad

DAIRY ▪ MAKES 12-15 SERVINGS ▪ NON-GEBROKTS

3 cups heavy whipping cream

8 ounces confectioner's sugar

5 Red Delicious apples, cored
  and diced with skin on

½-¾ cup raisins

¾ cup chopped walnuts

Until I tried this recipe, I never understood the appeal of Waldorf salad. Globs of mayonnaise with apple pieces floating in it is not my idea of haute cuisine. Try this incredible updated version, which substitutes heavy cream for the mayonnaise, for a salad even your kids will love. Serve it plain or on a bed of lettuce.

Whip the cream and sugar until stiff peaks form. Fold in apples and raisins. Sprinkle with walnuts.

Chef's Salad

MEAT ▪ MAKES 8-10 SERVINGS ▪ NON-GEBROKTS

DRESSING:

3 tablespoons mayonnaise

¼ cup olive oil

1½ teaspoons sugar

¼ teaspoon freshly
   ground black pepper

1 tablespoon chopped
   fresh parsley

1 tablespoon thinly
   sliced scallions

1 teaspoon imitation
   Dijon mustard

2 cloves fresh garlic, minced

juice of 1 lemon

SALAD:

¼ pound pastrami, sliced into
   thin strips

¼ pound smoked turkey
   breast, sliced into thin strips

¼ pound salami, sliced into
   thin strips

1 small red onion, thinly sliced

1 cup cherry tomatoes

1 pound mixed salad greens

This recipe is a family favorite. I usually turn to it as part of the Passover Shabbos lunch. Since the protein is right in there, it really is a main-dish salad.

In a jar or cruet, mix the mayonnaise, oil, sugar, pepper, parsley, scallions, mustard, garlic, and lemon juice. Shake or whisk until emulsified.

Toss the pastrami, turkey, salami, red onion, and tomatoes with the salad greens. Lightly coat with dressing.

Cucumber-Dill Salad

DAIRY ▪ MAKES 6-8 SERVINGS ▪ NON-GEBROKTS

A classic — and no wonder! This recipe is quick, easy, cool, refreshing, and delicious. English (hothouse) cucumbers are usually sold wrapped in plastic at the supermarket. They are longer than other varieties and are said to be seedless, although I always scoop out the seeds when I am using them in a recipe. The skin is thin and not waxed, so it can be eaten.

Slice each cucumber in half lengthwise. With a melon baller or a spoon, scoop out and discard the seeds from each cucumber.

Cut each cucumber half into ¼-inch bias-cut slices. Place into a medium bowl.

Add the sour cream, salt, dill, lemon juice, and red onion slices. Toss to combine.

Transfer to a chilled bowl or salad plates.

3 English (hothouse) cucumbers, peeled

¾ cup sour cream

1½ teaspoons fine sea salt

2 tablespoons chopped fresh dill

juice of ½ large lemon, or 1 tablespoon lemon juice

½ small red onion, very thinly sliced

Watermelon and Yellow Beet Salad

PARVE ▪ MAKES 6 SERVINGS ▪ NON-GEBROKTS

3 large yellow beets, peeled, or 1 ripe mango

½ medium seedless watermelon, about 3 pounds when weighed with the rind

2 tablespoons extra-virgin olive oil

juice of 1 lemon, about 2 tablespoons

1 tablespoon balsamic vinegar

2 teaspoons honey

¼ teaspoon fine sea salt

¼ teaspoon freshly ground black pepper

3 ounces (about 6 cups) mesclun lettuce

7 fresh basil leaves

6 fresh mint leaves

Who else but Moshe David could make such a show-stopping presentation out of such basic ingredients? You will need a sturdy hand to make the beet balls. If you can't find yellow beets, mango works great too. Peel a mango, leaving it whole, but cut a thin slice off the bottom so it is sturdy on the work surface while balling it.

If using the beets, with a melon baller, scoop out round balls of beets. Place into a small pot of boiling water and cook until soft, about 9 minutes.

If using the mango, prepare as stated in the note above and make balls using a melon baller or rounded teaspoon measure.

Meanwhile, using the same size melon baller, scoop out balls of watermelon and set them aside, covered with a wet paper towel so they don't dry out.

Whisk olive oil, lemon juice, vinegar, honey, salt, and pepper. Add the mesclun and toss.

When the beets are soft, drain and add to the salad. Toss. Add the watermelon balls. Stack the basil leaves and thinly slice into ribbons. Mix into the salad, reserving some for the top of each serving. Portion the dressed salad into 6 (6–8 ounce) martini glasses.

Garnish each glass with some of the remaining basil and a mint leaf.

Seared Ahi Tuna Niçoise

PARVE ▪ MAKES 6 SERVINGS ▪ NON-GEBROKTS

3 (8-ounce) ahi tuna steaks

fine sea salt

freshly ground black pepper

1 tablespoon olive oil, divided

6 ounces baby arugula or spring mix

3 tablespoons extra-virgin olive oil, plus more for drizzling

1 tablespoon lemon juice

1 small head Belgian endive, very thinly sliced

1½ cups grape tomatoes, halved

1 (7-ounce) jar Niçoise, Kalamata, or Gaeta olives, pitted and coarsely chopped

6 scallions, thinly sliced on the diagonal

fleur de sel or coarse sea salt

3 hard-boiled eggs, peeled and sliced lengthwise into quarters

To properly make hard-boiled eggs, place them into a small pot. Cover with cold water and bring to a boil over medium heat. When the water boils, cover the pot, turn off the heat, and allow the eggs to sit for 15 minutes.

Heat an empty grill pan or skillet over medium heat. Sprinkle both sides of each tuna steak with salt and pepper. Rub 1 teaspoon oil into each steak, spreading it evenly on both sides.

When the pan is hot, place the tuna into it and sear for 2–3 minutes per side; the tuna should still be pink inside. Do not overcook.

Place the arugula or spring mix into a medium bowl. Add 3 tablespoons extra-virgin olive oil, lemon juice, ½ teaspoon salt, and ½ teaspoon pepper. Toss to coat.

Place the lettuce onto 6 plates. Add endive and tomato halves. Sprinkle with chopped olives and scallions.

Slice the tuna into ¼-inch slices and arrange on the salads. Lightly drizzle the tuna with additional olive oil and sprinkle with fleur de sel or coarse sea salt.

Arrange the quartered eggs on the plates.

POULTRY

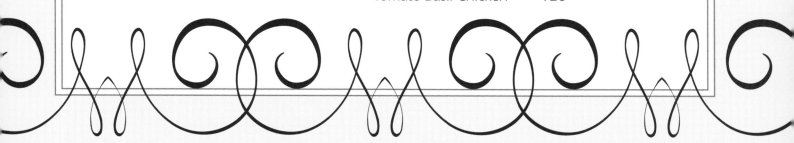

Cranberry Chicken

MEAT ▪ MAKES 4–6 SERVINGS ▪ NON-GEBROKTS

2 medium oranges

1 chicken, with bone and skin, cut into eighths

1 (16-ounce) can whole berry cranberry sauce

1 cup bottled French dressing

2 tablespoons dry onion soup mix

You will love this moist chicken dish. The combination of tart, tangy, and sweet, plus its gorgeous colors, will surely make it a keeper for all-year round.

Preheat oven to 375°F.

Zest 1 orange and reserve the zest. Slice the orange.

Slice the second orange and place all the orange slices in an even layer into a roasting pan.

Arrange the chicken skin-side-up on the oranges.

In a medium bowl, mix the cranberry sauce, dressing, and onion soup mix. Add the orange zest. Mix. Pour over the chicken, coating all the pieces.

Bake uncovered for 1½ hours. Transfer to a plate or serving platter along with the caramelized orange slices.

Ratatouille Chicken Stew

MEAT · MAKES 4-6 SERVINGS · NON-GEBROKTS

olive oil

1 chicken, cut into eighths, or 10 chicken thighs

1 small Asian eggplant, cut into ½-inch cubes, or 1 small Italian eggplant, peeled and cut into ½-inch cubes

2 carrots, peeled and cut into small chunks

1 onion, cut into small chunks

1 celery stalk, cut into small chunks

1 bay leaf

2 teaspoons dried thyme

1 teaspoon whole black peppercorns

2 shallots, thinly sliced

3 cloves fresh garlic, sliced

⅓ cup sliced black olives, optional

1 (13.5-ounce) can artichokes, drained

½ cup red wine

1 (28-ounce) can crushed tomatoes

2 roasted red peppers (jarred or fresh), sliced

fresh basil leaves, chopped, for garnish

Many people do not eat roasted meats at the Seder. Stews work well and can be the perfect answer when looking for an all-in-one main dish.

Preheat oven to 400°F.

Place 1 tablespoon olive oil into a very large Dutch oven or very large ovenproof sauté pan, or prepare in two batches in medium pans. When oil is hot, add the chicken pieces, skin-side-down. Sear skin until evenly golden. Flip the pieces to get color on the other side as well. The chicken will render out some fat. Remove the chicken pieces from the pan and set aside; do not drain off the oil.

Into the same frying pan, add the eggplant. Add olive oil as needed. Sauté for 3–4 minutes. Add carrots, onion, celery, bay leaf, thyme, and peppercorns. Sauté for 6–8 minutes, until onions soften. Add shallots and garlic; sauté until soft, 4–6 minutes. Add olives, if using, and artichokes. Add red wine. Shake the pan and then let the wine cook down to 2 teaspoons.

Add crushed tomatoes and roasted red peppers. Simmer for 5–10 minutes.

Bring to a low boil, and cook until the vegetables are soft, about 10 minutes.

Place chicken, skin-side-up, on top of the vegetables; do not submerge or skin will become rubbery.

Put into the oven, uncovered, for 50 minutes. Spoon some juices and vegetables over the chicken and bake for another 2 minutes. Garnish with fresh chopped basil.

Balsamic Herb-Rubbed Chicken

MEAT ▪ MAKES 8 SERVINGS ▪ NON-GEBROKTS

Preheat oven to 350°F.

In the bowl of a food processor fitted with a metal blade, place the basil, parsley, rosemary, thyme, vinegar, oil, mustard, salt, and red pepper flakes. Pulse until it forms a coarse herb paste.

Place chicken pieces into a baking pan and rub each piece with the paste, coating chicken completely.

Bake, uncovered, for 1½ hours. If skin doesn't look crisp, run the chicken under the hot broiler for 1–2 minutes. This dish can also be cooked on an outdoor grill.

½ cup firmly packed fresh basil leaves

½ cup chopped fresh parsley

2 tablespoons chopped fresh rosemary

2 tablespoons chopped fresh thyme

¼ cup balsamic vinegar

¼ cup olive oil

2 tablespoons imitation Dijon mustard

¾ teaspoon fine sea salt

¼ teaspoon crushed red pepper flakes

2 chickens, cut into eighths

Zesty Chicken

MEAT ▪ MAKES 8 SERVINGS ▪ NON-GEBROKTS

Preheat oven to 350°F.

Place the chicken, in a single layer, into a baking dish.

In a small mixing bowl, mix the mayonnaise, ketchup, and onion soup mix. Stir to combine.

Pour the dressing mixture over the chicken and spread it over each piece.

Place the baking dish into the oven and bake, uncovered, for 1 hour and 15 minutes, or until chicken is cooked through and no longer pink, or a meat thermometer inserted into the thickest part of the thigh reads 180°F. Transfer to a bowl or platter.

8 chicken parts, with bone and skin

½ cup mayonnaise

¼ cup ketchup

4 teaspoons dry onion soup mix

Roasted Garlic Chicken Stuffed with Dried Fruits and Nuts

MEAT ▪ MAKES 4 SERVINGS ▪ NON-GEBROKTS

1 head garlic

extra-virgin olive oil

fine sea salt

freshly ground black pepper

10-12 dried apricots

5 dried Mission figs

½ cup shelled, raw pistachio nuts (unsalted and not roasted)

1 whole (3-5 pound) chicken or pullet, washed and patted dry

½ orange, unpeeled, sliced

2 sprigs fresh rosemary

kitchen twine

3 tablespoons margarine, melted

You can prepare this dish with chicken parts as well. Lay the orange slices and sprigs of rosemary in your baking pan. Place the stuffed chicken pieces on top. Bake as directed below.

Preheat oven to 375°F.

Holding the head of garlic on its side, cut 1–2 inches off the top of the bulb to expose the cloves. Place the head into the center of a square of foil on a small baking pan. Drizzle with olive oil and season with salt and pepper. Close the foil packet. Roast for 45 minutes–1 hour until soft, golden, and fragrant.

Meanwhile, in a food processor fitted with a metal blade, chop the apricots, dried figs, and pistachios into very small pieces.

With your finger, loosen the skin of the chicken, going under the skin of the breasts, thighs, and legs.

Massage the fruit mixture under the skin, getting it into cavities where the skin was loosened.

Stuff orange slices and rosemary into the cavity of the chicken. Tie the legs closed with kitchen twine. Place the chicken on a rack in a roasting pan; try not to let too much of the fruit and nuts drip out into the pan or they will burn.

When the garlic is soft and caramelized, remove it from the oven and squeeze the roasted garlic from the skin onto a cutting board. Mash the garlic with the back of a knife to make a smooth paste. Rub it all over the outside of the chicken.

Drizzle the margarine over the top of the chicken, letting it run down the sides.

Tent with aluminum foil. Bake, covered, for 1 hour and 15 minutes, basting 2–3 times with the pan juices. Uncover and roast until the skin is brown, watching to make sure the garlic doesn't burn.

Cornish Hens with Pistachio Paste

MEAT ▪ MAKES 4 SERVINGS ▪ NON-GEBROKTS

2 cups raw, unsalted, shelled pistachio nuts, finely chopped, divided

4 (1-pound) baby Cornish hens, butterflied, backbone removed, pressed flat with your palm

fine sea salt

freshly ground black pepper

3-4 tablespoons olive oil

6 shallots, sliced

2 tablespoons fresh thyme or 2 teaspoons dried thyme

1½ cups chicken stock, plus a little extra as needed

4 basil leaves or other brightly colored flat leaves, for garnish

The pistachio paste can be served at room temperature, which makes this dish great for Shabbos lunch.

Preheat oven to 350°F.

Stuff ¼ cup chopped pistachio nuts under the skin of each hen. Massage the nuts under skin to help spread them out evenly. Salt and pepper both sides of each hen.

Heat olive oil in 2 large sauté pans (or plan to sear in batches). Sear the hens, skin-side-down, until golden brown. Remove hens from the pan and place into roasting pans in a single layer. Set aside. Add shallots to the sauté pan with the hen drippings. Sauté 6–7 minutes. Sprinkle in thyme. Deglaze the pan with chicken stock, using a wooden spoon to loosen any nuts stuck to the pan.

Meanwhile, place the hens, uncovered, in the oven. Roast for 30 minutes, or until done.

Prepare the pistachio paste: In a deep container, or in the bowl of a food processor fitted with a metal blade, place ½ cup chopped pistachio nuts. Add shallots and pan drippings. Using an immersion blender or food processor, blend into a paste. Thin with a little stock if needed.

Dollop a tablespoon or 2 of pistachio paste on a basil or other flat lettuce leaf; place at the side of the hen. Sprinkle all with remaining chopped pistachios.

Lemon-Pepper Fried Chicken

MEAT ▪ MAKES 6 SERVINGS ▪ GEBROKTS

4 boneless, skinless chicken breast halves

vegetable oil

1½ cups potato starch, divided

½ cup matzo meal

1 tablespoon coarse black pepper or 2 teaspoons finely ground black pepper

zest and juice of 1 lemon

1½ cups cold water

6-7 ice cubes

fine sea salt

1 cup mayonnaise

1 tablespoon chopped fresh dill or 1 teaspoon dried dill

A grown-up version of chicken fingers, this recipe will please eaters of all ages. The coating is a tempura batter that also works well for zucchini, red bell pepper strips, and eggplant.

Thinly slice the chicken into long, very thin, bias-cut strips. Set aside.

Pour oil into a heavy medium pot, filling it three-fourths of the way. Heat over medium to 350°F.

While the oil is heating, prepare the batter: Place ¼-cup potato starch into a shallow container. Set aside. In a medium metal bowl, whisk the remaining potato starch, matzo meal, black pepper, zest, lemon juice, and 1½ cups cold water. Add ice cubes, as tempura batter fries up better when it is cold.

Dip the chicken strips into the container of potato starch. Shake off excess. Add strips to the batter, coating well. Add more ice cubes as the ice melts.

Add coated chicken strips to the heated oil, a few at a time. Fry, until golden-brown, turning occasionally. If you under-brown the chicken, the starch will remain gummy. Remove with a slotted spoon and drain on paper towels. Sprinkle with salt.

In a small bowl or container, mix the mayonnaise with chopped dill, stirring to combine.

Serve the warm chicken strips with dill mayonnaise.

Pastrami-Stuffed Turkey Roast with Pineapple Glaze

MEAT ▪ MAKES 8-10 SERVINGS ▪ NON-GEBROKTS

1 (4-5 pound) boneless turkey roast, with skin, tied

¼ pound sliced pastrami

fine sea salt

freshly ground black pepper

garlic powder

onion powder

paprika

dried parsley flakes

2 tablespoons olive oil

kitchen twine

1 (20-ounce) can pineapple chunks in juice

A few years back ArtScroll ran a recipe contest for Kosher by Design Entertains. A friend of Miriam L. Wallach of Woodmere, N.Y. submitted some recipes on her behalf with the note that Miriam is one of the best and most creative cooks in her community. She bakes and distributes challahs every Shabbos for fun and relaxation. Enough said.

A cooking note: Turkey breast dries out very easily, so keep a close eye on the cooking time. If you are using a smaller roast, decrease the cooking time. If you have leftovers, don't reheat; just bring to room temperature.

Preheat oven to 350°F.

Untie the turkey breast. If in a plastic sleeve, discard the sleeve or it will burn when you sear the turkey. Slide your fingers under the skin to loosen it and make a pocket. Slide pastrami slices into this pocket.

Retie the turkey with kitchen twine. Liberally season both sides of the breast with salt, pepper, garlic powder, onion powder, paprika, and parsley.

Heat the olive oil in a large skillet. When the oil shimmers, add the turkey, skin-side-down. Allow to sear until skin is golden brown, 4–5 minutes. Turn and sear the other side for 4–5 minutes.

Transfer the turkey to a shallow baking dish that snugly holds it.

While the pan is still hot, add pineapple chunks with their juices. Turn heat to medium-low. Scrape up the browned bits. Simmer until the sauce becomes syrupy and pineapple turns an amber color, about 5–8 minutes. Pour this glaze over the turkey.

Bake 1½–1¾ hours. The turkey will continue to cook when removed from the oven.

Allow the turkey to rest for 15 minutes before slicing and serving.

Garnish with pineapple sauce.

Glazed Chicken Breasts with Strawberry Salsa

MEAT • MAKES 8 SERVINGS • NON-GEBROKTS

Season chicken with salt and pepper on both sides.

Heat oil in a medium skillet or grill pan over medium heat. Add chicken and sear on both sides, 4–5 minutes per side, until browned. You can also grill the chicken on a barbecue grill. Remove the chicken to a plate.

To the same pan, add the minced shallot and sauté on low heat until soft, about 4 minutes. (If you used a barbecue, heat 2 tablespoons olive oil in a pan, sauté the shallot in it, and continue.) In a small bowl, dissolve the potato starch in the chicken stock. Add it to the pan. Add jelly and balsamic vinegar. Cook until thickened, about 1–2 minutes. Return the chicken to the pan and coat both sides with the glaze. Remove from heat.

Prepare the salsa: Place the chopped strawberries into a small bowl. Toss with red onion, balsamic vinegar, pepper, mint, and lime juice. Allow flavors to blend for 10 minutes.

Serve chicken with the salsa, warm or at room temperature.

GLAZED CHICKEN BREASTS:

4 boneless, skinless chicken breast halves, tenders removed

fine sea salt

freshly ground black pepper

2 tablespoons olive oil

1 shallot, minced

1 teaspoon potato starch

½ cup chicken stock

3 tablespoons strawberry jelly

1½ tablespoons balsamic vinegar

STRAWBERRY SALSA:

2 cups fresh strawberries, chopped

2 tablespoons chopped red onion

1½ tablespoons balsamic vinegar

¼ teaspoon freshly ground black pepper

1 tablespoon chopped fresh mint

juice of 1 lime

Coq au Vin

MEAT ▪ MAKES 6-8 SERVINGS ▪ NON-GEBROKTS

4 chicken thighs, with skin

4 chicken legs, with skin

4 chicken breasts, with skin

fine sea salt

freshly ground black pepper

1 bottle good-quality Cabernet Sauvignon

3 tablespoons olive oil, divided

2 cups wild mushrooms (oysters, shiitake, cremini), just caps, discard stems

1 medium carrot, peeled and cut into chunks

1 large onion, cut into chunks

1 cup chicken stock

2 tablespoons potato starch

4 tablespoons water

It is best to marinate the chicken in the wine the night before. It will really soak up t flavor of the wine and the color will be magnificent.

Season chicken pieces on both sides with salt and pepper. Place into a large container in a single layer. Pour the wine to cover the chicken and place uncovered in the refrigerator overnight.

The next day, remove the chicken pieces from the container, reserving the wine marinade.

Preheat oven to 325°F.

Place 2 tablespoons of oil into a large frying pan over medium-high heat. Add chicken pieces, skin-side-down, in batches. Sear the chicken on both sides until nice and brown. The sugars from the wine will help caramelize the skin quickly.

As the chicken pieces are done, remove them to a baking dish, skin-side-up. To the same pan, add mushrooms and 1 tablespoon olive oil. Sauté for 2 minutes. Add the carrot and onion. Season with salt and pepper. Sauté for 2 minutes, until nice and shiny. Add 1 cup of wine marinade and chicken stock to deglaze the pan.

Pour the mushroom mixture and wine over the chicken. Loosely cover and bake for 1½ hours.

When the chicken is done, strain the juices into a medium pot. In a small bowl, whisk potato starch with water. Bring the juices to a boil. Reduce heat to low. Whisk in the potato starch slurry and return to a boil. The mixture will thicken. Stir. Simmer for 5 minutes. Pour the sauce back over the chicken.

Orange Chicken

MEAT • MAKES 6-8 SERVINGS • NON-GEBROKTS

This is an old family recipe from my Aunt Temmie, a real New England lady who is great in the kitchen. She raised her four children in Tivertown, a small town in Rhode Island, where the entire population is well under 10,000! It was hard to keep kosher there and she had to drive to Boston or Providence to find kosher butchers. Once there, she stocked up on chicken and meat so that she could prepare favorite family dishes like this one.

If your pans don't fit into your oven side by side, you may need to bake the lower pan for an extra few minutes so that the orange slices will caramelize.

Preheat oven to 375°F.

Place the chicken pieces in single layers, skin-side-up, into two 9- by 13-inch baking pans.

In a medium bowl, with a fork, mix brown sugar, nutmeg, and potato starch. Stir in the orange juice. Pour half the mixture over each pan of chicken.

With the back of a spoon, spread the top of each chicken piece with the marmalade.

Scatter paper-thin slices of orange over chicken, leaving some skin exposed.

Bake, uncovered, for 1 hour. Baste with the pan juices and bake for an additional 15–20 minutes or until the oranges are a deep amber color and the chicken is fully cooked and no longer pink, or a meat thermometer inserted into the thickest part of the thigh reads 180°F. Transfer to a bowl or platter.

- 2 chickens, cut into quarters
- ¾ cup dark brown sugar
- ¼ teaspoon ground nutmeg
- 2 tablespoons potato starch
- 1 cup orange juice (not from concentrate)
- 1 (12-ounce) jar orange marmalade
- 2 navel oranges, very thinly sliced

Citrus and Garlic-Crusted Duck Breasts

MEAT ▪ MAKES 8 SERVINGS ▪ NON-GEBROKTS

4 boneless duck breasts, with skin

zest of 1 lemon

zest of 1 orange

6 cloves roasted garlic (see note) or ½ teaspoon garlic powder mixed into a paste with ¼ teaspoon water

3 sprigs flat leaf parsley, leaves finely chopped, stems discarded

Here is a quick method for roasting garlic. Once you know how to make it, you can use it in hundreds of dishes. Place whole, peeled cloves of garlic in a small pot. Add olive oil to cover. Bring to a boil over medium-low heat. Gently boil for 5 minutes (the garlic may turn golden-brown). Remove from heat. Allow to stand in the oil for 20 minutes. The garlic will be soft and caramelized. The oil can be stored in an airtight non-metal container in the refrigerator for 3 weeks and used anywhere olive oil is called for; the garlic flavor infuses into the oil, adding a wonderful taste.

Preheat oven to 350°F.

Trim excess fat from the duck breasts. Score the skin, making deep diamond-shaped cut marks through the layers of fat, but be sure not to cut into the duck meat. Heat an empty frying pan over medium heat. Place the duck skin-side-down into the hot pan. Allow the fat to render out, pouring it off as it releases. It will take about 15 minutes for all the fat to render out and for the skin to get browned and crisp. Turn over and cook for 4 minutes on the other side.

Using a sharp knife, finely chop the lemon zest, orange zest, roasted garlic, and parsley. Keep going over it with a knife, chopping and smearing with the back of a knife until it is a smooth paste.

Gently spread the citrus paste over the skin side of each duck breast to form a crust.

Bake for 10 minutes.

Allow the duck to rest for a few minutes. Slice on the diagonal into ¼-inch slices. Serve over a bed of greens or matzo farfel. Using matzo farfel will make this dish gebrokts.

Kishka-Stuffed Chicken

MEAT ▪ MAKES 6 SERVINGS ▪ GEBROKTS

When I was growing up my family went out to the deli for dinner on many Sundays. One of the delicacies we would order was kishka, which came smothered in gravy. I still use kishka in my cholent, so there is always one in my freezer. It is a wonderful creamy filling in this chicken dish. The bright orange color is eye-catching.

Preheat oven to 350°F.

Place each chicken breast between 2 sheets of waxed paper or parchment paper. Using a rolling pin or meat pounder, pound to an even ¼-inch thickness.

Cut a 1-inch slice of kishka. Roll it into a log and place into the center of a flattened cutlet. Repeat with the remaining 5 chicken breasts. You may have leftover kishka. Roll the cutlets around the kishka, tucking in the ends.

Pour the matzo meal, salt, pepper, and brown sugar into a plate or bowl. Add the olive oil and toss with your fingers to combine.

Brush each chicken roll with 1 tablespoon apricot preserves and dip into matzo meal, coating all sides. Place the chicken rolls, seam-side-down, into a baking pan.

Lightly drizzle each roll with honey.

Bake, uncovered, for 30 minutes. Allow to stand for 10 minutes. Lightly drizzle with more honey. Serve whole or sliced.

6 boneless, skinless chicken breast halves

1 kishka, defrosted, all casings removed

1 cup matzo meal

1½ teaspoons fine sea salt

1 teaspoon freshly ground black pepper

2 teaspoons light brown sugar

1 tablespoon olive oil

6 tablespoons apricot preserves

honey

Fiesta Turkey Burgers

MEAT ▪ MAKES 6 SERVINGS ▪ NON-GEBROKTS

1 pound ground white-meat turkey

1 pound ground dark-meat turkey

1 tablespoon lime juice

1 teaspoon fine sea salt

½ teaspoon freshly ground black pepper

1 teaspoon dried oregano

1 teaspoon garlic powder

1 tablespoon vegetable oil

1 red onion, very thinly sliced

1 ripe Haas avocado, peeled, pitted, and thinly sliced

store-bought salsa

My girlfriend Karen Finkelstein gave me a fabulous time-saving tip. When she brings home various meats from the butcher, she seasons them as per recipes she plans on using and then freezes them, labeled with the recipe title. This allows her to defrost meat that is ready to go into the oven. This recipe would be a perfect candidate for this time-saving technique. Season the mix of ground turkey, form the patties, and freeze. On a day when time is short, just pop them into the fridge in the morning and grill them right before dinner. Such a simple and smart idea!

In a medium mixing bowl, combine the white-meat turkey, dark-meat turkey, lime juice, salt, pepper, oregano, and garlic powder.

Divide the meat into 6 equal portions and form into patties. Set aside.

Pour the vegetable oil into a grill pan or medium skillet. Heat the pan over medium heat. Add burgers to pan. Cook 5 minutes per side. Try not to move the burgers around on the grill pan so you will get nice grill marks.

Assemble the burgers: Place a few slices of red onion on top of each turkey burger. Add a few slices of avocado. Top with some salsa.

Primavera Chicken

MEAT • MAKES 8 SERVINGS • NON-GEBROKTS

"Primavera" is the Italian word for "spring." Tomatoes are not at their best yet in the spring, but the long roasting process of this recipe caramelizes them so that they taste sweet and delicious.

Preheat oven to 350°F. Place the chicken pieces in single layers, skin-side-up, into two 9- by 13-inch baking pans.

Slice the squash and zucchini in half lengthwise and then slice into 1-inch-thick half-moons. Scatter over the chicken. Toss on the halved tomatoes.

Shake the dressing and drizzle it over the chicken.

Bake, uncovered, for 1½ hours.

Remove the chicken to a platter. Toss the vegetables in the pan liquid and then scatter them over the chicken.

8 chicken parts, with bone and skin

1 yellow squash, unpeeled

1 green zucchini, unpeeled

1 quart cherry tomatoes, halved

1 (8-ounce) bottle Italian dressing

Greek Garlic Chicken

MEAT ▪ MAKES 6-8 SERVINGS ▪ NON-GEBROKTS

2 chickens, cut into eighths

2 onions, cut into large chunks

2 lemons

12-16 sprigs fresh oregano

8 cloves fresh garlic, halved

fine sea salt

freshly ground black pepper

½ cup olive oil

1 cup white wine

1½ cups Kalamata olives, pitted and coarsely chopped

½ cup Kalamata olives, whole, for garnish

Pitting Kalamata olives is a breeze. Just smack each olive with your palm and the pit pops right out. If you don't have Kalamata olives, you can use canned black olives, but the Kalamata are more authentic and richer-tasting.

I garnish this delicious dish with some of the ingredients used to flavor it, such as fresh oregano sprigs and whole olives. It brings some of those vibrant colors back to the dish.

Preheat oven to 450°F.

Place the chicken pieces in single layers, skin-side-up, into two 9- by 13-inch baking pans.

Add the onion chunks. Slice the lemons in half lengthwise. Squeeze the lemon halves over the chicken. Cut each lemon half into 4 pieces; add to the chicken.

Set aside 4 sprigs of oregano and strip the oregano leaves from the rest. Scatter the leaves and the stripped sprigs over the chicken; they will add their perfume to the dish.

Add the garlic and season with salt and pepper. Drizzle with the oil and wine. Toss the mixture together. Sprinkle the chopped olives over the chicken.

Bake, uncovered, for 45 minutes – 1 hour, or until chicken is fully cooked and no longer pink, or a meat thermometer inserted into the thickest part of the thigh reads 180°F.

Transfer to a platter and garnish with whole olives and reserved oregano sprigs.

Mediterranean Poached Chicken

MEAT ▪ MAKES 6 SERVINGS ▪ NON-GEBROKTS

6 boneless, skinless chicken breast halves, pounded very thin

fine sea salt

freshly ground black pepper

2 tablespoons olive oil

½ red onion, very finely diced

⅛ teaspoon ground turmeric

pinch of cayenne pepper

pinch of dried rosemary, crumbled

1 medium russet potato, peeled and cut into small cubes

1 red bell pepper, seeded and finely diced

1 green bell pepper, seeded and finely diced

1 rib celery, finely diced

2 cups chicken stock

½ cup Pinot Grigio or other white wine

zest and juice of 1 lemon

¼ cup pitted green Spanish olives, coarsely chopped

GARNISH:

1 tablespoon olive oil

1 lemon sliced into 6 slices

This healthful winner is reminiscent of a stew, except it cooks very quickly. The gorgeous color comes from turmeric, which is the same spice that gives ballpark mustard its yellow color.

Season the chicken with salt and pepper. Roll one chicken breast lengthwise into a long cylinder. Secure with 3 toothpicks and slice into thirds to yield 3 equal spirals. Keep the toothpicks in place. Repeat with the other 5 breasts.

Heat the oil in a large pot over medium heat. Add the red onion; sauté for 2 minutes. Add the turmeric, cayenne, rosemary, and potato cubes. Sauté for 3–4 minutes, stirring with a wooden spoon. The starch from the potato will make it stick to the pot. Add the red bell pepper, green bell pepper, and celery. Pour in the stock and white wine. Add the juice and zest of the lemon. Bring to a simmer. Add the secured chicken spirals. Cover and simmer for 10–15 minutes, or until the chicken is no longer pink.

Season with salt and pepper. Sprinkle in chopped olives.

To garnish this dish: Heat 1 tablespoon of olive oil in a small skillet over medium heat. Add the lemon slices and sear until they start to brown.

Remove and discard the toothpicks. Serve 3 spirals with the vegetables and some of the broth. Garnish with a seared lemon slice.

Honey and Pecan-Crusted Chicken with Apricot Chutney

MEAT ▪ MAKES 6 SERVINGS ▪ GEBROKTS

APRICOT CHUTNEY:

1 (16-ounce) jar duck sauce

1 cup dried apricots, chopped

HONEY & PECAN-CRUSTED CHICKEN:

nonstick cooking spray

½ cup honey

¼ teaspoon fine sea salt

¼ teaspoon freshly ground black pepper

½ teaspoon paprika

2 teaspoons garlic powder

1½ cups matzo meal

¾ cup chopped pecans

6 boneless, skinless chicken breasts, pounded flat to an even thickness

When cutting dried fruit, spray your knife blade with nonstick cooking spray. This will prevent the fruit from sticking to the knife.

Combine the duck sauce with the chopped apricots. Let the chutney sit for at least an hour.

Preheat oven to 400°F.

Lightly spray a cookie sheet with nonstick cooking spray.

In a medium bowl, combine the honey, salt, pepper, paprika, and garlic powder. Whisk to combine. In a shallow dish, combine the matzo meal with the pecans.

Brush the chicken cutlets with the honey mixture and then dredge in the pecan mixture. Place in a single layer in the prepared pan; spray the tops with cooking spray. Bake for 20 minutes.

Serve the chicken with the apricot chutney.

Artichoke Chicken

MEAT • MAKES 6 SERVINGS • NON-GEBROKTS

This chicken gets a thumbs-up from friends and relatives for its taste and aroma. I give it two thumbs-up for ease. If you want to double the recipe, just make the recipe twice. You won't be able to fit 12 cutlets into a skillet in one batch anyway. You don't have to clean the pan between batches, but this will ensure that all the chicken will have the amazing garlic flavor. If you prepare the dish in advance and reheat, cook the chicken just until it's no longer pink. Don't overcook or it will be dry when reheated.

In a large skillet, melt the margarine. Add half the garlic and cook for 1 minute over medium heat. Add the chicken and cook 4–6 minutes per side or until cooked through. Remove to serving platter.

Place the oil into the same skillet. Add the remaining garlic and cook 1 minute. Add the mushrooms and cook for 3 minutes. Use a spatula to scrape up the browned bits. Add the artichokes; cook for 1 minute. Add the wine and lemon juice. There won't be much liquid, but bring it to a boil. Lower the heat and simmer for 5 minutes. Use the spatula to gently break the artichoke hearts into chunks. Pour the mushrooms and artichokes over the chicken. Serve immediately.

- 3 tablespoons margarine
- 8 cloves fresh garlic, minced, divided
- 6 boneless, skinless chicken breasts, pounded to an even thicknesss
- 1 tablespoon olive oil
- 8 ounces sliced mushrooms
- 1 (14-ounce) can artichoke hearts, packed in water, drained, or hearts of palm, sliced
- 2 tablespoons white wine
- 1 tablespoon fresh lemon juice

Slow-Roasted Rotisserie Chicken

MEAT • MAKES 4 SERVINGS • NON-GEBROKTS

Once a month I mix up a huge batch of this seasoning mixture and keep it in a jar with my spices. This cuts my preparation time to under a minute each time I make this dish, and it is often! It is my kids most-requested chicken dish. I make mine on a small rotisserie but have gotten equally great results using this low and slow oven-cooking method.

Preheat oven to 300°F.

In a small bowl, mix the salt, garlic salt, pepper, brown sugar, cayenne, paprika, onion powder, and barbecue seasoning.

Rub the spice mix all over the skin of the chicken. If time permits, place the chicken into the refrigerator, uncovered, for 2–3 hours or up to overnight; this will help the skin crisp.

Place the chicken on a rack in a baking dish. Roast for 2 hours at this low temperature. During the last hour of cooking time, baste every ½ hour with the pan juices.

- ½ teaspoon coarse sea salt or kosher salt
- ½ teaspoon garlic salt
- ¼ teaspoon black pepper
- 1 teaspoon dark brown sugar
- ¼ teaspoon cayenne pepper
- ½ teaspoon paprika
- ¼ teaspoon onion powder
- 1 teaspoon barbecue seasoning (check ingredient list for hickory or mesquite flavoring)
- 1 (3-5 pound) whole chicken

Chicken Provence
with Cider-Roasted Vegetables

MEAT ▪ MAKES 6 SERVINGS ▪ NON-GEBROKTS

3 beets, peeled and cut into wedges

3 Idaho potatoes, peeled and cut into chunks

3 parsnips, peeled and cut into 2-inch chunks

1½ cups baby carrots

2 large Vidalia onions, cut into chunks

4 tablespoons dark brown sugar

4 tablespoons olive oil

2 tablespoons apple-cider vinegar

1 whole chicken

3 tablespoons margarine, softened at room temperature

¾ teaspoon dried tarragon leaves

¾ teaspoon dried rosemary leaves, slightly crushed

½ teaspoon dried oregano

½ teaspoon freshly ground black pepper

½ teaspoon dried thyme leaves

2 teaspoons chopped flat leaf parsley

paprika

This bountiful dinner of perfectly roasted chicken and root vegetables is so simple to prepare.

Preheat oven to 450°F.

Place beets, potatoes, parsnips, carrots, and onions into a large roasting pan.

In a medium bowl, whisk together brown sugar, oil, and vinegar. Pour mixture over the vegetables and toss to coat well. Place the chicken, breast-side-down, in the center of the roasting pan (it can be on top of some of the vegetables).

Place softened margarine into a small bowl. Sprinkle in the tarragon, rosemary, oregano, pepper, thyme, and parsley. Using a spoon, stir the herbs into the margarine so they are evenly distributed into a paste.

Using your fingers, gently lift the skin of the chicken and rub some of the herbed margarine under the skin. Rub remaining margarine evenly over the outside of the chicken.

Generously sprinkle with plenty of paprika, rubbing into the skin of the chicken. Place in the oven, uncovered, and roast for 1 hour.

Lower the heat to 350°F. Stir the vegetables. Flip the chicken over and sprinkle the top of the chicken generously with paprika. Roast for another 15 minutes. Remove from oven and let stand 10 minutes before serving.

Chicken with Brandy and Mushrooms

MEAT ▪ MAKES 6 SERVINGS ▪ NON-GEBROKTS

It's very easy to double this recipe. You need a skillet large enough to hold 2 cut-up chickens and sauce. If you don't have a large skillet, you can brown the chicken in batches and then place the pieces into a large roasting pan. Double the sauce, following the directions below, but instead of placing the chicken back into the pan, pour the sauce over the chicken pieces in the roasting pan. Then bake in a 350°F preheated oven uncovered for 1½ hours, basting every 15 minutes.

In a very large skillet over medium heat, heat vegetable oil to depth of ½-inch. Season the potato starch with salt and pepper. Dredge the chicken pieces in the potato starch. Shake off the excess.

When oil is hot enough (it should bubble when you dip a wooden toothpick or skewer into it), brown the chicken on both sides; remove from pan. Set aside.

Discard most of the oil. Add the garlic and sauté 3 minutes. Add the thyme leaves, brandy, wine, stock, mushrooms, turkey, and tomato paste; bring to a boil.

Return the chicken to the pan. Lower the heat. Cover and simmer for 1 hour.

Transfer to a serving dish.

vegetable oil

potato starch

fine sea salt

freshly ground black pepper

1 chicken, cut in eighths, skin removed

3 cloves fresh garlic, 2 chopped and 1 minced

2 sprigs fresh thyme, stems removed

¼ cup brandy

⅓ cup red wine

½ cup chicken stock

4 ounces sliced mushrooms

⅓ pound or 6 ounces cooked smoked turkey, cubed

2 teaspoons tomato paste

Poached Chicken in Leek Broth

MEAT ▪ MAKES 6 SERVINGS ▪ NON-GEBROKTS

4 leeks, divided

6 boneless, skinless chicken breast halves

2 bay leaves

2 teaspoons coarse sea salt or kosher salt

8 whole black peppercorns

juice of 2 lemons

3 sprigs fresh parsley

1 cup white wine

chicken stock or chicken consommé powder dissolved in water

This is a very beautiful and healthy dish. The leek ribbons make each cutlet look like a perfectly wrapped present. Complement the colors of the white chicken and green leeks by serving them atop a one- or two-tone vegetable purée.

Cut the very bottom from 2 of the leeks. Separate each leek into individual long leaves. Clean the leaves. Using a sharp knife, cut each leaf in half so you have long, ½-inch wide ribbon-like strips.

Pour water to depth of 1-inch into a large pot; bring to a boil. Drop the leek ribbons into the boiling water and blanch for 30 seconds or until leek is softened; quickly remove from the water.

Lay 2 leek ribbons to form a plus sign. Place a chicken cutlet in the center. Tie each ribbon around the cutlet, knotting in the middle. Use scissors to trim any long pieces. Repeat process for all 6 cutlets. Place the chicken in a single layer in a large pot or heavy skillet. Slice the other 2 leeks into ½-inch strips. Scatter them over the chicken. Add the bay leaves, salt, peppercorns, lemon juice, parsley sprigs, and wine. Add enough chicken stock to cover the chicken.

Bring the liquid, uncovered, to a boil over high heat. Reduce heat to medium and poach for 15 minutes or until chicken has lost its pink color. If the tops of any of the packets are exposed, spoon some of the poaching liquid over them as they cook.

Vegetable Purée

MEAT ▪ MAKES 8 SERVINGS ▪ NON-GEBROKTS

2½ pounds fresh cauliflower florets, chopped

5 cloves fresh garlic, sliced

1⅔ cups chicken stock

2½ teaspoons kosher salt

8 tablespoons nondairy creamer

5 teaspoons margarine

freshly ground black pepper

You will get rave reviews on this healthy, low-carb substitute for whipped potatoes. It turns a simple vegetable into a delicious and visually appealing treat. The recipe is written for cauliflower, but can be prepared with carrots as well. Just use 8 peeled and sliced carrots and let simmer longer.

In a large pot, place the cauliflower, garlic, chicken stock, and salt. Bring to a boil. Cover and reduce to medium heat. Simmer about 10 minutes or until cauliflower is very tender.

Transfer the pot contents to the bowl of a food processor fitted with a metal blade. Add the nondairy creamer and margarine. Process until smooth. Season with black pepper.

Roast Turkey with Caramelized Onion-Balsamic Gravy

MEAT ▪ MAKES 12-15 SERVINGS ▪ NON-GEBROKTS

ROAST TURKEY:

- 4 tablespoons olive oil
- 1 teaspoon fine sea salt
- 1 teaspoon freshly ground black pepper
- 1 tablespoon paprika
- 1 tablespoon garlic powder
- 3 tablespoons apricot rib sauce or duck sauce
- 1 (10- to 14-pound) turkey, fresh or defrosted
- 8-10 ounces apricot nectar or pineapple juice

GRAVY:

- 6 cups chicken stock
- turkey neck and giblets (optional)
- 1 onion, quartered
- 1 bay leaf
- 6 tablespoons margarine
- 2 large onions, halved and thinly sliced
- 1 teaspoon dried rosemary
- 1 teaspoon dried sage
- ¼ cup potato starch
- ½ cup balsamic vinegar

I love this turkey recipe. The key is the gravy, which rewards all your efforts with a creamy, rich taste. For ease, it can be started the day before or when you put the turkey up to roast. You won't want to wait for the holidays to use this recipe.

Preheat oven to 400°F.

Make a paste out of the olive oil, salt, pepper, paprika, garlic powder, and apricot rib sauce.

Rub the spice mixture all over the turkey. Place turkey, breast side down, in a large roasting pan. You can sprinkle on more of the pepper, paprika, and garlic powder, if desired. Let turkey come to room temperature for 20 minutes. Bake 2 hours, covered.

Lower the temperature to 350°F and uncover. Turn turkey breast side up, being careful not to prick skin. Bake 1 hour.

Flip turkey over again and baste with apricot nectar or pineapple juice every 15 minutes for ½–1 hour. Turkey is done when juices run clear when pierced with a fork. Place turkey on serving platter; reserve liquid in pan for gravy.

Prepare the gravy: Combine the chicken stock, turkey giblets if desired, quartered onion, and bay leaf in a pot. Simmer about 1 hour or until reduced to 3 cups of liquid, skimming the surface if necessary.

In a large skillet, melt margarine over medium-high heat. Add sliced onions, rosemary, and sage and sauté about 15 minutes or until onions are golden. Add potato starch; stir 1 minute. Gradually whisk in chicken stock mixture, discarding bay leaf, turkey neck, and quartered onion. Boil about 3 minutes or until the gravy thickens, stirring often. Whisk in the vinegar.

Rewarm the gravy and thin with more chicken stock if necessary. Pour over sliced turkey or serve on the side.

Crispy Chicken Lollipops

MEAT ▪ MAKES 6 SERVINGS ▪ GEBROKTS

CHICKEN LOLLIPOPS:

- 1 cup Manischewitz Italian Herb Coating Crumbs
- 4 whole matzo boards
- 1 teaspoon dried thyme
- ½ cup fresh minced parsley
- ½ cup matzo cake meal
- 3 large eggs, lightly beaten
- 6 boneless, skinless chicken breast halves
- 3 scallions, ends trimmed, cut into 2-inch lengths, white and pale green parts only
- vegetable oil

DIPPING SAUCE:

- 4 tablespoons mayonnaise
- 3 tablespoons apricot preserves
- 1½ teaspoons lime juice
- ⅛ teaspoon fine sea salt
- ⅛ teaspoon freshly ground black pepper
- ⅛ teaspoon ground turmeric

Preheat oven to 400°F.

Soak 6 wooden skewers in water. Set aside.

Place the Herb Coating Crumbs into a shallow container large enough to accommodate the skewers. Place the matzo boards into the bowl of a food processor fitted with a metal blade. Pulse until crumbs form, being careful not to pulse too finely. Add to the coating crumbs with the thyme and parsley; toss to combine. Set aside.

Place the matzo cake meal in a second shallow container large enough to accommodate the skewers, and pour the beaten eggs into a third shallow container.

Place the chicken breasts horizontally on your cutting board. Cut each chicken breast, vertically, into 3 equal 2-inch rectangular chunks, trimming off any uneven ends. With the skewer piercing the center of the width of the scallion, thread on one scallion. Thread on a chicken chunk; repeat 2 more times and end with a scallion. Each skewer should have 3 chicken chunks and 4 scallions. Trim so they all line up to form a large rectangle, similar in size to a popsicle.

Working with 1 skewer at a time, dip the chicken into the cake meal, shaking off excess. Dip into the beaten eggs, and then into the container of herbed coating. Repeat with remaining skewers.

Fill a large skillet with ½-inch of oil. Heat over medium. Add the skewers in batches, cooking for 2 minutes per side until golden. Remove to a cookie sheet as they are done.

Place the chicken into the oven to finish cooking, about 5 minutes.

In a small bowl whisk the mayonnaise, apricot preserves, lime juice, salt, pepper, and turmeric. Serve the lollipops with the dipping sauce.

Teriyaki Chicken

MEAT ▪ MAKES 8-10 SERVINGS ▪ NON-GEBROKTS

2 chickens, with bone and skin, cut into eighths

½ teaspoon fine sea salt

¼ teaspoon freshly ground black pepper

¼ teaspoon chicken consommé powder

2 tablespoons olive oil

TERIYAKI SAUCE:

8 teaspoons beef consommé powder

2 cups cola, not diet

1 tablespoon vegetable oil

2 cloves fresh garlic, minced

1 (1½-inch) piece fresh ginger, peeled and minced

4 tablespoons sugar

2 tablespoons honey

1 tablespoon potato starch, dissolved in 1 tablespoon water

2 tablespoons cooking sherry

1 tablespoon chopped fresh chives or scallion, for garnish

This teriyaki is a sweet and sticky homemade sauce that is spiked with fresh ginger and garlic. It mimics real teriyaki so well, you will be looking for the take-out guy's delivery truck.

Preheat oven to 375°F.

Place the chicken in a single layer in a large roasting pan. In a small bowl mix the salt, pepper, and chicken consommé powder. Season both sides of each part with this mixture.

Heat the olive oil in a large skillet over medium heat. Add the chicken pieces, skin-side-down, and sear until the skin is golden. Do this in batches if necessary. Return the chicken to the pan, skin-side-up. When all the chicken is seared, place into the oven, and bake uncovered, for 30 minutes. Drain the liquid.

Meanwhile, prepare the teriyaki sauce: In a medium pot, dissolve the beef consommé powder in the cola. Simmer for 2 minutes. Remove from heat. In a medium pan, heat the vegetable oil. Sauté the garlic and ginger for 1 minute, until cooked through and starting to become golden. Add it to the cola. Add the sugar and honey. Whisk as it simmers for 1 minute. Whisk in the dissolved potato starch and simmer for 30 seconds–1 minute until thickened. Add the sherry. Remove from heat.

Glaze the chicken with the teriyaki, turn the pieces skin-side-down and return to the oven, uncovered for 25 minutes or until chicken is no longer pink inside. Transfer to a platter, arranging the pieces skin-side-up. Brush with the teriyaki from the pan and serve with extra sauce on the side. Garnish with chives or scallions.

Tomato-Basil Chicken

MEAT • MAKES 10-12 SERVINGS • NON-GEBROKTS

2 chickens, cut into eighths

2 large beefsteak tomatoes, cut into large chunks

1 (8-ounce) bottle Italian dressing

½ cup fresh basil leaves

4 cloves fresh garlic

5 sun-dried tomatoes, packed in oil

fresh basil leaves, for garnish

Besides tasting great, this chicken dish has a fabulous aroma. It will make your whole house smell amazing. The combination of the chopped tomatoes, garlic, and fresh basil give it some real eye-appeal, as well, which is sometimes hard to achieve with a chicken dish.

Preheat oven to 350°F.

Place the chicken pieces in single layers, skin-side-up, into two 9- by 13-inch baking pans. Set aside.

Place the chunks of tomato into a food processor fitted with a metal blade. Pulse to chop. Add the dressing, basil, garlic, and sun-dried tomatoes. Pulse to purée and emulsify.

Pour the tomato-basil dressing evenly over the chicken pieces.

Bake, uncovered, for 1 hour and 30 minutes or until chicken is fully cooked and no longer pink, or a meat thermometer inserted into the thickest part of the thigh reads 180°F.

Transfer to serving platter. Garnish with fresh basil leaves.

MEAT

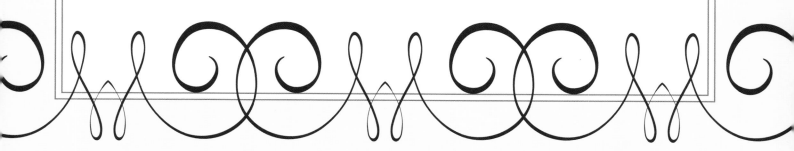

Veal Scallopini with Kumquats

MEAT ▪ MAKES 6 SERVINGS ▪ GEBROKTS

18 veal scaloppini, pounded paper-thin

fine sea salt

freshly ground black pepper

2 jars mini oranges or kumquats in syrup

1 large spaghetti squash

2 tablespoons margarine

½ cup Manischewitz Italian Herb Coating Crumbs

½ teaspoon dried thyme

⅓ cup fresh minced parsley leaves

2 whole matzo boards

½ cup matzo cake meal

3 large eggs, beaten

olive oil

The mini oranges in syrup, sometimes packaged as candied kumquats, are loved by gourmands around the world. They are pretty, sweet, and the thin rind is edible. The brand that Moshe David recommends is "Agam Hagalil Mini Oranges in Syrup" and is available on the internet at Israeliproducts.com if you can't find it in stores. You can also find it at igourmet.com.

If you can't find the jars of mini oranges, you can make your own. Place 1 cup sugar and 1 cup water into a medium pot. Cut both ends off of 36 fresh kumquats and add to the pot together with the juice of an orange, and a sprig of rosemary. Bring to a boil. Turn down the heat and simmer for 15 minutes. Allow the kumquats to marinate in the syrup in the refrigerator for at least a few hours and up to a week.

Arrange 3 slices of the veal vertically, in a slightly overlapping fashion to form a rectangle on a piece of plastic wrap. Cover with plastic wrap and use a meat pounder to flatten the veal paper-thin and help meld the 3 cutlets together. Make sure there are no gaps in the meat, as it will be rolled up as one sheet later in the recipe. Repeat with the other 5 batches of veal cutlets. Season with salt and pepper. Arrange a horizontal line of the oranges towards the bottom edge of each veal rectangle. Starting from the bottom and using the plastic wrap to help, roll each veal rectangle into a cylinder larger than a hot dog but smaller than a salami. Make sure the plastic doesn't get caught in the meat. Roll the plastic-wrapped cylinder in aluminum foil and place into the freezer for 20 minutes.

Meanwhile, prepare the spaghetti squash: Place the whole squash into a pot of water. Bring to a boil and cook for 40 minutes, until you can prick with a fork. Drain the water. Cut the squash in half lengthwise and discard the seeds. Carefully put the hot flesh back into the pot, separating the strands with a fork to form spaghetti-like strings. Add the margarine, season with salt and pepper. Heat to melt the margarine. Set aside.

Place the Herb Coating Crumbs into a shallow container. Add the thyme and parsley. Place the two matzo boards into the bowl of a food processor fitted with a metal blade. Pulse until crumbs form, being careful not to pulse too finely. Add to the crumbs and toss to combine. Set aside.

Place the matzo cake meal into a second shallow container and the beaten eggs into a third shallow container.

Remove the veal from the freezer and discard the foil and plastic wrap. Using both hands to support the roll and keep it from falling apart, dip the veal, one cylinder at a time, into the cake meal, shaking off excess. Dip into the beaten eggs, and then into the container of herbed coating.

Pour olive oil into a skillet to come up ½-inch on the skillet. Sear the veal rolls, carefully turning them with 2 wooden spoons as each side browns, about 3 minutes per side, until golden brown.

Place 3 mounds of spaghetti squash into the center of each plate. Slice each veal loaf on the diagonal into 3 pieces. Stand one piece on each bed of spaghetti squash. You may have extra squash.

Bloody-Mary-Marinated London Broil

MEAT ▪ MAKES 8 SERVINGS ▪ NON-GEBROKTS

1 large shoulder London broil, about 3 pounds

1 cup tomato juice

1 tablespoon lemon juice

1 tablespoon lime juice

1 tablespoon prepared white horseradish

2 cloves fresh garlic, minced

2 dashes cayenne pepper

½ teaspoon celery salt

½ teaspoon dried oregano

½ teaspoon fine sea salt

½ teaspoon freshly ground black pepper

olive oil

A Bloody Mary is a famous non-kosher-for-Passover cocktail containing vodka, tomato juice, and various spices and flavorings. Bartenders may guard their secret recipes, but most garnish the drinks with stalks of celery. It is one of the few cocktails that is enjoyed at a brunch table. This recipe takes the non-alcoholic ingredients of a traditional Bloody Mary and turns them into a fabulous marinade and sauce for steak.

Score the meat on both sides, making shallow diamond-shaped cuts. Set the meat into a shallow non-reactive baking dish, such as Pyrex or glass.

In a medium bowl, whisk the tomato juice, lemon juice, lime juice, horseradish, garlic, cayenne, celery salt, oregano, salt, and black pepper.

Pour the marinade over the meat and let stand at room temperature.

Meanwhile, grease a barbecue grill or grill pan lightly with olive oil and preheat it.

Remove the meat from the marinade, pouring the marinade into a small pot, and sear the meat for 10 minutes per side.

Meanwhile, heat the marinade over medium heat. Bring to a simmer for 3–5 minutes, until slightly thickened.

Allow the meat to rest for 10 minutes. Thinly slice on the diagonal. Serve the slices with the sauce on the side or drizzled over the top.

Dry Rub Short Ribs

MEAT ▪ MAKES 6 SERVINGS ▪ NON-GEBROKTS

2-3 large racks beef ribs, not cut into spare ribs, or flanken, leave fat on meat side (can always be trimmed later but you need it or the ribs will be dry), trim fat from bone side, allow 2 bones per person

3 tablespoons olive oil

coarse sea salt or kosher salt

freshly ground black pepper

2 carrots, unpeeled, cut in half

1 parsnip, unpeeled, cut in half

1 stalk celery, cut in half

3 cloves fresh garlic, peeled

1 onion, cut into quarters; leave end root attached so it stays together

¾ ounce fresh thyme or 1 teaspoon dried

1 bottle Syrah or other red wine

SPICE RUB:

1 tablespoon dried oregano

1 teaspoon ground cinnamon

1 teaspoon garlic powder

1 teaspoon onion powder

1 teaspoon paprika

½ teaspoon crushed red pepper flakes

½ cup dark brown sugar

The slow braise in wine makes these ribs melt-in-your-mouth delicious. They are great served over mashed potatoes.

In a large soup pot over medium heat, heat the olive oil.

Season both sides of ribs with salt and black pepper.

Sear meat on both sides until nicely browned; about 6–7 minutes per side.

When the meat is seared on both sides, add carrots, parsnip, celery, garlic, onion, and thyme. Add the wine. Add water to cover completely.

Reduce heat to medium-low and cover the pot. Slowly braise the ribs for 1½–2 hours. Remove the ribs from the pot. Cool. The recipe can be prepared in advance up to this point. When ready to serve, cut into individual portions.

You can cook the braising liquid, reducing it down to use for a gravy for this or another dish. You can also freeze it and use for beef stock.

Bring meat to room temperature. Prepare the spice rub: In a bowl, combine oregano, cinnamon, garlic powder, onion powder, paprika, crushed red pepper flakes, and brown sugar. Rub into the meat.

Get a large skillet very hot. Add a drizzle of olive oil. Sear the meat for just a few minutes; it is already cooked.

To serve, stack 2 for individual serving, or pile on a platter.

Balsamic Braised Brisket
with Shallots and Potatoes

MEAT ▪ MAKES 6 SERVINGS ▪ NON-GEBROKTS

1 (3-pound) beef brisket

fine sea salt

freshly ground black pepper

10 cloves fresh garlic, peeled, divided

3 tablespoons margarine, divided

2 tablespoons olive oil

3 Yukon Gold potatoes, peeled and cut into chunks

6 whole shallots, peeled

¼ cup balsamic vinegar

¼ cup red wine

1 (14½-ounce) can crushed tomatoes

Searing meat means exposing it to high heat to brown it on the surface. This seals in the flavor. It forms a crust which enables the meat to retain its juices.

Preheat oven to 400°F.

Season the brisket on both sides with salt and pepper. Using the tip of a sharp knife, cut shallow slits all along the brisket. Cut 5 of the garlic cloves in half. Place a piece of garlic into each slit. Place 2 tablespoons of the margarine and the oil into a large skillet or pot set over medium heat. When the margarine is melted and hot, add the meat. You should hear it sear on contact. Let it cook for 8 minutes — don't move it around. After 8 minutes, lift the meat up, add 1 tablespoon margarine to the pan, and turn the meat over. Sear on the second side for 8 minutes. Remove the brisket to a baking pan. Surround the brisket with the potatoes, shallots, and 5 whole garlic cloves.

Add balsamic vinegar and wine to the skillet or pan. Add the tomatoes. Turn the heat down to medium and cook for 5 minutes, stirring to combine. While the mixture cooks down, scrape up the browned bits from the pan; a wooden spoon works well here. Pour balsamic mixture over the brisket and vegetables. Add water to just cover the brisket.

Place in the oven and bake for 2–2½ hours, covered. Allow to cool before slicing.

Braised Rib Roast with Melted Tomatoes

MEAT ▪ MAKES 6-8 SERVINGS ▪ NON-GEBROKTS

This recipe is elegant enough to be the centerpiece of a formal dinner, but simple enough to follow using single rib steaks. If making with rib steaks, cut the eye away from the bone and discard the bone. Reduce the oven cooking time to 20 minutes. After cooking, slice the steak into strips and serve.

Preheat oven to 450°F.

Season the rib roast with salt and pepper. Heat the oil in a large ovenproof pot or Dutch oven. Add the roast to the hot oil, turning to sear evenly on all sides, about 3–4 minutes per side. Try not to manipulate the meat while it is searing. The meat will release itself when it is properly seared.

Add the onions, garlic, and tomatoes to the pot. Add the thyme leaves. Sauté 3–4 minutes. Add water to come up halfway on the roast.

Place the pot, uncovered, into the oven for 1 hour and 30 minutes, until thermometer inserted in center reads between 150° and 160°F. Remove the roast from the oven and let stand for 10 minutes.

Serve with the tomatoes and onions from the pot.

1 (5- 6-pound) standing beef rib roast

fine sea salt

freshly ground black pepper

4 tablespoons olive oil

2 onions, coarsely chopped

4 cloves fresh garlic, cut into chunks

2 beefsteak tomatoes, cut into large chunks

6 sprigs thyme, remove leaves, discard stems

Lamb Chops with Parsley Pesto

MEAT ▪ MAKES 6 SERVINGS ▪ NON-GEBROKTS

2 cloves fresh garlic

1 teaspoon fine sea salt

1 teaspoon dried rosemary

¼ teaspoon ground cayenne pepper

1 cup loosely packed fresh mint leaves

1 cup loosely packed fresh parsley leaves

1 tablespoon plus 1 teaspoon lemon juice (can be bottled)

½ cup olive oil

18 baby lamb chops

This delicious green sauce can just as easily go over sliced steak or chicken, but the hints of mint, garlic, and rosemary really complement lamb beautifully. If you have a mini-food processor, it will work even better than a full-sized one to really grind the ingredients to a good, thick paste.

Preheat broiler to high.

In the bowl of food processor fitted with a metal blade, pulse the garlic, salt, and rosemary. Add the cayenne, mint leaves, parsley leaves, and lemon juice. Pulse. With the machine running, slowly pour in the olive oil and allow the mixture to fully combine.

With a flexible spatula, transfer one-third of the pesto to a small bowl and reserve for serving after the chops are cooked. Pour the rest into a second bowl.

Place the lamb chops on a broiler pan. Lightly brush both sides of the lamb chops with the pesto.

Broil the lamb chops, 6–8 inches from the heat, for 7 minutes. Turn the lamb chops over and broil for another 3 minutes.

To serve, place 3 lamb chops on each plate with a dollop of the reserved parsley pesto.

Easy Meat Roast

MEAT ▪ MAKES 8-10 SERVINGS ▪ NON-GEBROKTS

4 pound California roast, beef brisket, or shell roast

1 large onion, sliced into rings

5 cloves fresh garlic, minced

½ cup ketchup

½ cup barbecue sauce

3 tablespoons brown sugar

This dish is so easy, even children can make it, lending a hand to holiday cooking.

Preheat oven to 350°F.

Place the meat into a heavy baking pan that is just big enough to hold it. Spread the onion rings over the meat. Scatter minced garlic over the meat.

Pour the ketchup, barbecue sauce, and brown sugar into a small bowl. Stir to mix. Pour over the meat.

Cover the pan with aluminum foil and place into oven for 2½ hours.

When the meat is done, carefully remove it from the oven. When it is cool enough to handle, carefully slice it thinly. You can reheat it in the sauce.

Shepherd's Pie

MEAT ▪ MAKES 6-8 SERVINGS ▪ NON-GEBROKTS

3 tablespoons olive oil

1½ onions, cut into ¼-inch dice

16 baby carrots, sliced, or 2 regular carrots cut into ¼-inch slices

2 stalks celery, sliced into ¼-inch pieces

4 cloves fresh garlic, chopped

¼ teaspoon fine sea salt

¼ teaspoon freshly ground black pepper

1 sprig fresh thyme

1 bay leaf

1 (28-ounce) can whole peeled tomatoes

2 pounds ground beef (can use ½ ground turkey and ½ ground beef)

1 teaspoon sugar

1 teaspoon beef or chicken consommé powder

leftover mashed potatoes or fresh mashed potatoes from 2 large Idaho potatoes mashed with 1 tablespoon margarine, salt, and 1 tablespoon nondairy creamer

What to do with leftover mashed potatoes, leftover chopped meat, leftover vegetables? How about the ultimate comfort food? It's right out of my childhood: Shepherd's Pie. If you don't have leftover mashed potatoes, just peel some Yukon Gold, russet, or Idaho potatoes, cut into chunks, and boil. When soft, mash with some salt, pepper, and nondairy creamer. Don't mash in a food processor or they will become gluey, but the job can be done in a Kitchen Aid stand mixer with a whisk attachment.

If the occasion calls for a more formal presentation, divide the filling among individual ramekins before piping with potatoes and baking. To make the potatoes easier to pipe, add a little more creamer.

Preheat oven to 425°F.

Heat the oil in a large frying pan over medium heat. Add the onions, carrots, and celery. Sauté 3–4 minutes. Add the garlic. Add the salt and pepper. Add the leaves from the sprig of thyme and the bay leaf.

Lift the tomatoes out of their liquid and drain well. Chop and add to the pan. Add the ground beef and sauté until brown, about 12–15 minutes. Remove the bay leaf and discard it.

Add the sugar and consommé powder.

Place the meat mixture into a medium ovenproof casserole dish. Cover with mashed potatoes. For a decorative touch, you can pipe the mashed potatoes through a large star tip of a pastry bag.

Place in oven and bake for 20–30 minutes, until potatoes are just starting to brown.

Beef Roulade on Creamy Parsnips

MEAT ■ MAKES 6 SERVINGS ■ NON-GEBROKTS

2½ pounds eye of the rib
   steak; have butcher thinly
   slice and pound into 6
   flat pieces (as for veal
   scallopini), tied

½ teaspoon fine sea salt

¼ teaspoon freshly ground
   black pepper

½ teaspoon garlic powder

½ teaspoon dried thyme

2 tablespoons olive oil

½ cup beef stock (can
   be made from beef
   consommé powder)

4 cups water

2 bay leaves

2 sprigs fresh rosemary

1 cup red wine, such as
   Cabernet Sauvignon

4 teaspoons potato starch

CREAMY PARSNIPS:

3 large parsnips, peeled and
   cut into ½-inch chunks

3 tablespoons margarine,
   cut into chunks

⅓ cup nondairy creamer

The perfect restaurant meal at home. Beautifully cooked tied rolls of beef atop a creamy mound of parsnips and drizzled with a wonderful red-wine sauce. If you are not so adventurous, feel free to leave out the creamy parsnips and just make the beef roulades. You can even roll 3–4 scallions into each roll for a negemaki-style roll. Save any remaining red-wine sauce, as it is the same recipe as used in the Sliced Beef with Cherry Brandy Sauce (see recipe on page 156). The extras can be the base for your next smashing meal, without the time or work.

Unroll each beef roll. Season with salt, pepper, garlic powder, and thyme. Re-roll and re-tie.

Heat the olive oil in a large skillet over medium heat. Sear the meat roulades, turning with tongs as they brown, for a total of 6–7 minutes.

Place the beef stock and water into a large soup pot. Whisk and bring to a boil. Add the bay leaves and rosemary. Reduce heat and simmer. When the roulades are seared, add them to the beef stock. Simmer for 10 minutes for medium-rare, or 12 minutes for medium, but do not overcook.

Remove the roulades from the stock. Discard rosemary and bay leaves. Whisk the red wine with the potato starch. Add to the stock. Simmer for 18–20 minutes until thick and syrupy.

Prepare the parsnips: Meanwhile, place the parsnips into a medium pot. Cover with water. Bring to a boil and cook until very soft, about 20 minutes. Drain the parsnips and place them, while hot, into the bowl of a food processor fitted with a metal blade. Add the margarine and creamer. Pulse until creamy and smooth, like mashed potatoes.

Place a dollop of creamy parsnips in the center of each plate. Slice each roulade in half and place the 2 halves on the parsnips. Drizzle with red-wine sauce.

Hazelnut- and Honey-Crusted Veal Chop

MEAT ▪ MAKES 6 SERVINGS ▪ NON-GEBROKTS

1½ cups shelled hazelnuts

1 clove fresh garlic, sliced

1 shallot, sliced

4 tablespoons honey

2 tablespoons chopped fresh chives, plus extra chives for garnish

6 (1½-inch thick) veal chops

fine sea salt

ground white pepper

This elegant dish is worthy of breaking out a nice bottle of white wine such as Chardonnay or a light red like a Pinot Noir.

Preheat oven to broil.

In the bowl of a food processor fitted with a metal blade, process the nuts, garlic, and shallot until finely minced. Add the honey and pulse to make a paste. Stir in the chopped chives. Set aside.

Season the veal chops on both sides with salt and white pepper.

Place the veal chops on a baking tray 6 inches from the heat and broil 5 minutes per side.

Spread a layer of the honey paste over one side of each veal chop. Place crust-side-up on the baking tray.

Return the tray, uncovered, to the oven on the rack farthest from the heat. Broil for 10 minutes longer, checking to make sure the honey crust is not burning.

Garnish with chives.

Herb-Crusted Silver Tip Roast

MEAT ▪ MAKES 8 SERVINGS ▪ NON-GEBROKTS

1 shallot, peeled and quartered

4 cloves fresh garlic, peeled

4 teaspoons olive oil

2 teaspoons dried thyme

2 teaspoons dried sage

3 teaspoons kosher or coarse sea salt

1½ teaspoons ground black pepper

1 (4- to 5-pound) silver tip roast, tied

Preheat oven to 400°F.

In the bowl of a food processor fitted with a metal blade, chop the shallot and garlic. Add the oil. Pulse 1–2 times. Remove the garlic mixture to a small bowl. Add the thyme, sage, salt, and pepper. Stir to combine.

Pat the meat dry with paper towels. Place into a roasting pan. Rub the meat all over with the herb paste.

Cover and chill 2–3 hours. (If you skip this step, reduce the cooking time. During the last 15–20 minutes, cut into the meat to make sure it is not becoming well-done.)

Bake, uncovered, for 30 minutes. Lower heat to 350°F. Bake for 1½ hours or until desired degree of doneness. Don't cook longer than 2½ hours or the meat will toughen. Also, keep in mind that the meat will continue to cook for about 15 minutes after you take it out of the oven.

Let meat stand for 15–20 minutes before slicing. The juices will return to the center of the roast, making it moist and easier to carve.

Sweet-and-Sour Brisket

MEAT ▪ MAKES 10 SERVINGS ▪ NON-GEBROKTS

1 (5-pound) beef brisket

1 (32-ounce) jar sauerkraut, partly drained

1 (28-ounce) can whole, peeled tomatoes

1 (16-ounce) box dark brown sugar

So simple yet so delicious, this dish is perfect when you have no time to fuss in the kitchen.

Preheat oven to 350°F.

Place the brisket into a roasting pan.

Pour the sauerkraut over the brisket. Add the tomatoes with their liquid. Sprinkle with the brown sugar. Cover with foil and bake for 3 hours.

Allow to cool before slicing. Reheat in sauce.

Pot Roast

MEAT ▪ MAKES 8 SERVINGS ▪ NON-GEBROKTS

When you exited the elevator in my mother-in-law's building, you were led by the nose to her doorway. The aroma of something great always wafted down her hallway. Her impromptu feasts didn't require a special occasion, just a butcher order and knowing that friends or family might be stopping by. This pot roast was one of my favorite dishes that she prepared. It's so tender that you can cut it with a fork. If unexpected guests arrive, you can always toss in a few extra carrots and potatoes to stretch the meal.

Pot roast involves browning beef and then braising it, covered in liquid, for several hours on the stove. This moist cooking process tenderizes the meat. Inexpensive cuts of meat work best. I am not sure why pot roast has dropped off the radar screen of younger cooks, but when you try this recipe you'll rediscover why our mothers and grandmothers prepared it so often.

In a large pot or Dutch oven, heat the olive oil and margarine. When the oil is hot but not smoking, sear the roast on all sides until golden brown. Remove from pot; set aside.

Add the sliced onion to the pot. Sauté about 5–6 minutes or until translucent, scraping up the brown bits from the pot as it sautés.

Return the roast to the pot. Add water to cover two-thirds of the way up the roast. Sprinkle with the dry onion soup mix. Bring to a boil. Reduce to a low simmer; cook, covered, for 2 hours. After 2 hours, turn the pot roast over. Add the carrots, potatoes, and parsnips. Re-cover and cook for another 1–1½ hours. Transfer meat to cutting board and let rest for 5 minutes. Slice meat. Place on platter with the vegetables. Serve with either jarred prepared horseradish or bottled barbecue sauce.

2 tablespoons olive oil

1 tablespoon margarine

1 (5-pound) boneless roast, such as shell roast

1 onion, sliced

1½ packages dry onion soup mix (from a 2¾-ounce box)

3 carrots, peeled and sliced, or 2 cups baby carrots

3 Idaho potatoes, peeled and cut into chunks

2 parsnips, peeled and cut into chunks

prepared horseradish or store-bought barbecue sauce

Stuffed Veal Roast

MEAT ▪ MAKES 6 SERVINGS ▪ NON-GEBROKTS

5 medium white button mushrooms

½ (10-ounce) box frozen chopped spinach, defrosted

3 sprigs fresh rosemary

10 ounces large pimiento-stuffed green olives

zest of 1 orange

zest of 1 small lemon

1 (3-pound) veal roast, netted and tied

fine sea salt

freshly ground black pepper

2 tablespoons olive oil

2 tablespoons honey

6 tablespoons apricot preserves

2 teaspoons imitation mustard

This show-stopping presentation is for wowing guests when you only have a few minutes to prep and get something into the oven. Make sure you have butcher's twine on hand for tying the roast.

Preheat oven to 375°F.

Place the mushrooms, the ½-box defrosted spinach, leaves from the rosemary sprigs, olives, orange zest, and lemon zest into the bowl of a food processor fitted with a metal blade. Pulse to combine to a paste.

Untie the roast. Season both sides with salt and pepper. Spread the stuffing paste evenly over the surface of the veal, generously covering it.

Reroll the roast and tie it just tightly enough to secure; don't tie too tightly or the filling will all ooze out. The filling will be visible.

Heat the olive oil in a large skillet. Add the veal roast and sear on all sides until the meat is a deep golden-brown. Place the seared roast into a roasting pan.

In a small bowl, mix the honey, apricot preserves, and mustard. Rub all the meat surfaces with a thick coating of the apricot-honey mixture, reserving some mixture. Bake for 1 hour, covered. Remove the roast from the oven and baste with remaining apricot-honey mixture. Return to the oven, uncovered, for 15 more minutes. Allow the roast to stand for 10 minutes before slicing. The roast should be juicy and slightly pink in the center.

Rack of Lamb with Fig-Marsala Sauce

MEAT ▪ MAKES 6 SERVINGS ▪ NON-GEBROKTS

4 tablespoons olive oil, divided

2 teaspoons dried rosemary

2 teaspoons dried thyme, minced

2 shallots

2 racks baby lamb chops, 9 chops per rack; have butcher French the bones

1 cup marsala wine, divided

8 fresh Mission figs or 6 dried figs, cut into quarters

½ cup chicken stock

This is my all-time favorite way to prepare lamb. I save it for special occasions and always receive accolades from my family and friends. Its dramatic presentation makes for an incredible dinner that is sure to impress. The fig sauce turns a gorgeous amber color. The flavors come together in a way that makes you feel like you've just dined in the most expensive restaurant, without ever leaving your driveway.

Preheat oven to 450°F.

In a food processor fitted with a metal blade, process 2 tablespoons olive oil, rosemary, thyme, and shallots 30–45 seconds, or until a thick paste forms.

Rub the herb paste into the lamb. Heat 2 tablespoons olive oil in a medium oven-proof skillet. Add the lamb, fat side down, and cook over high heat for 5 minutes. Turn the lamb and cook for an additional minute so that both sides are brown.

Add ½ cup wine to the skillet. Place the skillet in the oven and roast for 18 minutes. If your skillet is not oven-proof, cover the handles with foil.

Remove the skillet from the oven. Place the lamb on a platter; cover with foil to keep warm. Add the remaining ½ cup of wine and the figs to the skillet. Bring to a simmer. Use a spatula to loosen the brown bits from the pan. Add the stock and simmer for 3–4 minutes. The sauce will thicken and become a nice amber color. Pour sauce over the lamb and serve.

Roasted Shoulder of Veal in Mushrooms

MEAT ▪ MAKES 8 SERVINGS ▪ NON-GEBROKTS

1 (4- to 5-pound) boneless shoulder veal roast, rolled and tied in butcher string

coarse sea salt or kosher salt

freshly ground black pepper

4 cloves fresh garlic, peeled and coarsely chopped, divided

15 dried porcini or other dried mushrooms (about ½-1 ounce)

4 tablespoons margarine

2 tablespoons vegetable oil

3 onions: 2 cut into rings, 1 chopped

3 tablespoons potato starch

½ cup white wine

3 bay leaves

1 ounce dried crimini mushrooms or other dried mushrooms, soaked in ¾ cup hot water

2 tablespoons imitation mustard

I got this recipe from my friend's mother-in-law. The night that I prepared it for a taste-testing party, I listed it on the evaluation form as Mrs. Ratzker's Veal Roast. This dish was the hit of the evening. One taster commented, "I know Mr. Ratzker and now I know why he's always smiling."

Rub the veal with salt and pepper. Make 15 (1-inch deep by 1-inch long cuts) along the top and sides of the roast. Stick a garlic piece and a piece of dried mushroom into each cut.

In a large pot, melt the margarine and add the oil. Add the onion rings and fry them over medium-low heat for 15 minutes or until soft and golden, stirring occasionally to keep them from sticking to the pot. Remove the onions from the pot.

Rub the potato starch all over the veal.

Turn the heat up slightly. Place the veal into the pot. Make sure the veal sizzles when it hits the pot; if it doesn't, your oil is not yet hot enough. Brown the veal on all sides, about 4–5 minutes per side. If the roast sticks a little, it will release itself when the moisture is gone and the meat is properly sealed. If it is really sticking, then your heat is too high; turn the heat down just slightly.

Add the remaining garlic and the chopped onion; cook until wilted, about 2–3 minutes. Add back the onion rings. Add the wine and bay leaves.

Discard stems from the reconstituted mushrooms. Add mushroom caps and the liquid they were soaking in to the pot.

Turn the heat to low and cook, covered, for 2 hours. Turn the veal over a few times during cooking.

When the roast is done, remove it from the pot. Discard bay leaves. Add the mustard to the gravy and onions in the pot and mix well.

Place the veal back into the pot or transfer the gravy and the veal to a disposable tin. Let the roast cool completely. Refrigerate and slice when cold. If you slice while it's warm, it will fall apart. Rewarm the sliced veal with the gravy and serve.

Beef Bourguignon

MEAT ▪ MAKES 6-8 SERVINGS ▪ NON-GEBROKTS

2½-3 pounds large, well-marbled beef cubes, patted dry

3 tablespoons potato starch

2 tablespoons olive oil

1 (1-pound) bag frozen pearl onions or 2 onions, coarsely chopped

⅓ cup tomato paste

6 cloves fresh garlic, minced

1 tablespoon beef consommé powder dissolved in 2 cups very hot water

1 cup Burgundy or other full-bodied red wine

1 teaspoon dried rosemary, crumbled

1 teaspoon dried thyme

1 teaspoon dried parsley

¼ teaspoon fine sea salt

¼ teaspoon freshly ground black pepper

2 teaspoons potato starch for thickening gravy, optional

A wonderful version of a traditional French beef stew. Serve it over a mound of mashed potatoes. It is warm, filling comfort food at its best. This stew is even better the next day.

After the beef cubes have been patted dry, place them into a ziplock bag. Add the potato starch and toss to coat.

Heat the oil in a very large pot. Shake excess potato starch from the beef cubes and place them into the pot in a single layer, working in batches if necessary. Sear until brown on all sides, about 3 minutes per side. If done in batches, return all meat to the pot.

Add the pearl onions, tomato paste, and garlic. Stir to distribute. Brown and caramelize over medium heat about 4–5 minutes, stirring often.

Pour in the beef consommé and wine. Sprinkle in the rosemary, thyme, parsley, salt, and pepper.

Cover and simmer over low heat for 1½ hours.

If you like thicker gravy, transfer the meat and onions to a serving platter. Add the potato starch to the pot and whisk. Bring to a simmer over medium heat, whisking until thickened. Pour the gravy over the beef.

Sliced Beef
with Shiitake and Cherry-Brandy Sauce

MEAT ▪ MAKES 6 SERVINGS ▪ NON-GEBROKTS

¼ cup beef stock (can be made from beef consommé powder)

2 cups water

1 bay leaf

1 sprig fresh rosemary

½ cup red wine, such as Cabernet Sauvignon

2 teaspoons potato starch

1 (15-ounce) can sweet dark pitted cherries, with liquid

2 pounds London broil or filet split

fine sea salt

freshly ground black pepper

3 tablespoons olive oil, divided

8 shiitake mushroom caps

2 tablespoons brandy

The fruity sauce really elevates this simple steak into something spectacular. The sauce can be made in advance, making this palate-pleaser a winner for even the busiest cook.

Place the beef stock and water into a medium pot. Whisk and bring to a boil. Add the bay leaf and rosemary. Reduce heat and simmer for 15 minutes. Discard rosemary and bay leaf. Whisk the red wine with the potato starch. Add to the stock. Add liquid from the cherries, reserving cherries. Simmer for 20 minutes.

Meanwhile, season both sides of the beef with salt and pepper. Heat 2 tablespoons of the oil in a large skillet over medium heat. Sear the meat, 8–10 minutes per side. Allow to rest for 10 minutes before slicing on the diagonal into thin slices.

In the same skillet, heat the remaining tablespoon olive oil. Sear the shiitake caps until soft, about 3–4 minutes per side.

When the red-wine sauce is done, stir in the cherries and brandy. Simmer for 3 minutes to cook out some of the alcohol and heat through.

Serve the shiitake atop the steak slices and drizzle with the cherry-brandy sauce.

Beef Short Ribs with Horseradish

MEAT ▪ MAKES 6-8 SERVINGS ▪ NON-GEBROKTS

5 pounds beef short ribs

5 tablespoons potato starch, divided

3 tablespoons olive oil

1 onion, sliced into thick rings

2 carrots, peeled and thickly sliced

1 rib celery, sliced

2 cups beef stock or broth (can be made from beef consommé powder)

1 (28-ounce) can chopped tomatoes; if using whole canned tomatoes, drain, seed, and chop them

1 cup red wine

1 bouquet garni of 6 parsley stems, 3 sprigs fresh thyme, and 1 bay leaf (see note on page 50)

2 cloves fresh garlic: 1 chopped and 1 minced

1 tablespoon tomato paste

6 teaspoons bottled white horseradish, divided

freshly ground black pepper

chopped fresh parsley, for garnish

Beef short ribs are a kind of flanken, just longer and a little meatier. If you can't get them, regular flanken will do; just use strips that are as thick as possible and cut them into 3- to 4-inch pieces. This dish can be made in advance; it gets even better when reheated.

Preheat oven to 350°F.

Dredge the short ribs in 4 tablespoons potato starch.

In a large pot, heat the oil over medium-high heat. Get the oil hot enough so that the meat sizzles when added. If your oil is heated to the right temperature, the meat will sear on contact. Add meat in a single layer; you will need to do this in 2–3 batches. Brown the meat well on both sides, about 3–4 minutes per side.

Remove the meat from the pot. Reduce the heat to medium. Add the onion, carrots, and celery. Cook about 7–9 minutes, scraping up the brown bits as the onions caramelize.

Return the short ribs to the pot. Sprinkle with the remaining tablespoon potato starch, stirring to coat.

Add the beef stock, tomatoes, wine, bouquet garni, chopped and minced garlic, and tomato paste.

Raise the heat and bring to a simmer. Add 2 teaspoons of the horseradish and mix. Cover the pot and place it in the oven.

Simmer, stirring occasionally, until the meat is tender, about 2 hours. Just before serving, add the remaining horseradish and season with pepper. Sprinkle with parsley for garnish.

FISH/DAIRY

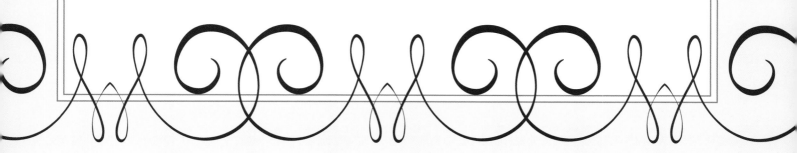

Tower of Snapper and Eggplant

PARVE ▪ MAKES 6 SERVINGS ▪ NON-GEBROKTS

2 pounds large red snapper fillets, cut into 12 (2-inch) strips on a bias

1 Asian eggplant, with skin, sliced into ½-inch rounds

fine sea salt

freshly ground black pepper

olive oil

2-3 beefsteak tomatoes, sliced into 12 (½-inch) slices

1 tablespoon margarine

¼ cup white wine

1 plum tomato, seeded, chopped into tiny dice

6 fresh basil leaves, finely chopped

instant mashed potato flakes

My photographer, John Uher, tells me that the current trend in his field is "tall" food. Well, this tower fits the bill with its elegant stack of brightly flavored layers.

Season the snapper and eggplant slices with salt and pepper.

Heat ¼-inch olive oil in a large skillet over medium heat. Sauté the eggplant slices until they turn golden, about 2–4 minutes, flipping a few times to get even color on both sides. Remove the eggplant; set aside. Carefully add the tomato slices to the skillet and sauté for 2–3 minutes until they begin to caramelize but do not get too soft. Remove from pan. Discard most of the oil, leaving just a coating in the pan. Add the margarine to the pan. When it is melted, add the wine and the snapper, skin-side-up. Cook for 2–3 minutes per side until cooked through; do not overcook.

Place the tomato dice and chopped basil into a small pot. Cover with olive oil. Bring to a simmer over low heat. Cook for 3 minutes once it achieves a simmer.

Prepare instant mashed potato flakes according to package directions to yield 4 servings.

Secure the tower by placing a large dollop of instant mashed potatoes into the center of each plate. Top with a piece of eggplant. Top with a tomato slice and snapper piece. Repeat, ending with snapper. You should have 2 snapper pieces, 2 tomato slices, and 2 eggplant slices in each tower.

Surround each tower with the simmered tomato dice.

Chardonnay Poached Salmon

DAIRY ▪ MAKES 6 SERVINGS ▪ NON-GEBROKTS

POACHED SALMON:

- 1 tablespoon butter
- 4 cups Chardonnay
- 1 shallot, chopped
- 6 sprigs fresh dill
- 2 teaspoons fine sea salt
- 1 teaspoon freshly ground black pepper
- 6 (6-ounce) salmon fillets, skin removed
- 2 tablespoons minced fresh dill

CHARDONNAY CREAM SAUCE:

- ½ cup chopped shallots
- 1 cup Chardonnay
- 1½ cups heavy cream
- 4 tablespoons (½ stick) butter, cut into pieces
- ½ teaspoon fine sea salt
- ¼ teaspoon freshly ground black pepper

Poaching involves partially or completely submerging the fish in a gently simmering liquid. This makes it almost impossible to dry out even the most delicate fish. When poaching, try to maintain a bare simmer; a more vigorous boil may cause the food to fall apart or cook unevenly. Poaching is done on a stovetop. If you have a long, narrow fish poacher, you will need to use a front and back burner at the same time.

You can serve this salmon fresh, but it is even better if you cover and refrigerate the poached salmon for at least 3 hours or up to a day. Let stand at room temperature for ½ hour before serving.

Kosher white wines have greatly improved over the past few years. You will need a full 750 ml bottle. If you can, splurge for a better bottle. The lower-priced wines taste acidic in this recipe.

Poached Salmon: Grease a fish poacher or a large, straight-sided sauté pan with 1 tablespoon butter. Add the wine, shallot, dill, salt, and pepper. Bring to a boil over high heat. Reduce the heat to medium and gently simmer for 5 minutes.

Add the salmon fillets to the poacher or pan. Sprinkle minced dill on top of the salmon. Spoon the liquid over the fillets. Cook, uncovered, about 10–15 minutes or until the salmon is firm and cooked through; may need longer if the fillets are thicker in the middle. Spoon the liquid over the fillets as they gently simmer in the poaching liquid. You will see the fillets become a lighter color as they become fully poached. Using a slotted spatula, remove the fillets from the pan.

Chardonnay Cream Sauce: Combine the shallots and wine in a saucepan. Bring to a boil and cook about 6 minutes or until most of the liquid has evaporated. Add the heavy cream, bring to a boil, lower the flame, and simmer about 3–4 minutes or until cream thickens and is reduced by almost half. Whisk in the 4 tablespoons butter. Season with salt and pepper. Serve sauce over salmon.

Pecan-Crusted Grouper over Amaretto Whipped Potatoes

DAIRY • MAKES 5 SERVINGS • NON-GEBROKTS

5 Yukon Gold potatoes, peeled, and cut into equal-sized chunks

fine sea salt

5 (6-ounce) grouper or salmon fillets

imitation Dijon mustard

¾ cup finely chopped pecans

4 tablespoons (½ stick) butter

⅛ cup heavy cream, warmed in microwave for 20 seconds

3 tablespoons amaretto liquor or pancake syrup

For a non-alcoholic version, use pancake syrup in place of the amaretto liquor.

Preheat oven to 375°F.

Place the potatoes into a large pot. Add water to cover and a large pinch of salt. Bring to a boil. Simmer for 15 minutes or until potatoes are easily pierced with a fork.

Meanwhile, prepare the fish: Lightly brush each fish fillet with the mustard. Press the pecans into the fish, making sure to cover all surfaces except the skin side. Place skin-side-down on a baking pan and bake for 15–20 minutes, until done.

Drain the potatoes, reserving ½ cup of the cooking liquid in case the potatoes turn out dry. Transfer to a large mixing bowl. Add butter, cream, and amaretto. Mash the potatoes with a potato masher or ricer. When well-mashed, whip for 1–2 minutes with an electric mixer set at medium speed. Add reserved cooking liquid if needed. Season with salt.

Serve the fish over a dollop of the whipped potatoes.

Halibut with Zucchini Confit

PARVE ▪ MAKES 4 SERVINGS ▪ NON-GEBROKTS

Preheat oven to 400°F.

Using a microplane, zest the lemon, being sure to get only the yellow part, not the bitter white pith. Set aside, reserving the lemon as well.

Brush the halibut with olive oil. Season both sides with salt and pepper.

Heat a heavy ovenproof skillet over medium heat until hot. Add the fish and sear for 1 minute per side until golden on each side. Place the skillet into the hot oven and roast until just cooked through, about 4–5 minutes.

Carefully remove the fish from the pan; the pan handle will be hot. Add 1 teaspoon olive oil to the pan. Add the zucchini. Cook over medium heat until soft; don't brown it. Season with salt and pepper and add water.

Add the reserved lemon zest, lemon juice, and thyme. Sauté 30 seconds. Top the halibut fillets with the zucchini confit.

1 medium lemon

4 (6-ounce) halibut fillets, skin removed

olive oil

fine sea salt

freshly ground black pepper

1 small zucchini, with skin, cut into ¼-inch dice

1 tablespoon water

1 teaspoon fresh thyme

Cod, Potatoes, and Sun-Dried Tomatoes

PARVE ▪ MAKES 6 SERVINGS ▪ NON-GEBROKTS

⅓ cup extra-virgin olive oil

2 pounds Yukon Gold potatoes, skin on, cut into ¾-inch dice

fine sea salt

freshly ground black pepper

1 teaspoon dried oregano, divided

1 cup homemade oven-roasted tomatoes (see below) or store-bought sun-dried tomatoes

2 cups vegetable stock

½ cup potato starch

2 pounds cod fillet, boneless and skinless

3 tablespoons olive oil

1 tablespoon vegetable oil

1 cup dry white wine, such as Chardonnay

1 cup black Niçoise or Kalamata olives, pitted and chopped

The easiest way to pit olives is to smack them against the work surface with the palm of your hand. The pit will pop right out.

Heat the oil in a large sauté pan over medium heat. Add the potatoes and sauté. Season with salt and pepper. Add ½ teaspoon oregano. When the potatoes begin to brown, add the tomatoes and stock. Simmer until the potatoes are tender, about 10 minutes. Set aside.

Place the potato starch into a plate. Coat the cod with the potato starch, shaking off the excess. Season both sides with salt and pepper. In a separate large pan, heat the olive oil and vegetable oil over medium heat. Add cod to the pan. Cook until golden brown, flipping fish once, about 5 minutes per side.

Remove the potatoes and tomatoes to your plates or platter. Place the cod on top of this mixture.

Add the wine and remaining ½ teaspoon of oregano to the pan in which you cooked your fish. Scrape up the browned bits with a wooden spoon. Turn the heat to medium-high and simmer for 3 minutes. Pour over the fish. Sprinkle with chopped olives.

Oven-Roasted Tomatoes

PARVE ▪ MAKES 6 SERVINGS ▪ NON-GEBROKTS

7 medium-large plum tomatoes

⅛ cup extra-virgin olive oil

3-4 cloves fresh garlic, peeled

leaves of 2-3 sprigs fresh thyme, or 2 teaspoons dried

fine sea salt

freshly ground black pepper

Preheat oven to 200°F. Cut the tomatoes in half lengthwise. Using a spoon, scrape out and discard seeds. Place the scooped-out tomatoes into a large bowl. Toss with the oil, garlic, thyme, salt, and pepper. Place the tomatoes cut-side-down on a parchment-lined baking sheet. If you have a broiling pan or baking rack that can be set on the baking sheet, use it so air will circulate. Place the baking sheet in the top third of the oven. Flip the tomatoes after 2 hours or the insides will steam and stew instead of drying out. Roast for a maximum of 6 hours. Remove from oven. When cool, slice into long strips. Can be made up to 1 week in advance and kept in an airtight container in the refrigerator.

Almond-Crusted Sole
with Strawberry-Mango Salsa

DAIRY OR PARVE ▪ MAKES 6 SERVINGS ▪ GEBROKTS

ALMOND-CRUSTED SOLE:

olive oil

12 sole fillets

fine sea salt

freshly ground black pepper

1 cup slivered almonds

¼ cup matzo meal

4 tablespoons (½ stick) butter or margarine, microwaved for 15 seconds

STRAWBERRY-MANGO SALSA:

1 mango, pitted, cut into ¼-inch dice

12 strawberries, stemmed, cut into ¼-inch dice

2 tablespoons balsamic vinegar

1 tablespoon extra-virgin olive oil

¼ teaspoon fine sea salt

1 shallot, minced

12 fresh mint leaves, thinly sliced, for garnish

This dish combines the quintessential summer flavors of strawberry and mango in a light salsa. When I make this dish, I always prepare extra salsa to serve warm as a light dessert over a scoop of dairy or parve vanilla or strawberry ice-cream.

Preheat oven to 350°F.

Brush the broiler pan with olive oil. Season each sole fillet with salt and pepper.

Place the almonds into a tall, quart-sized container. Add ¼ teaspoon salt and ¼ teaspoon pepper. With an immersion blender, pulse the almonds. This can also be done in a food processor fitted with a metal blade. Don't grind them too fine; you want to leave some texture. Add the matzo meal. Toss to mix. Mix the softened butter or margarine into the almonds to make a paste.

Place 2 fillets together, one on top of the other, and place on the prepared pan. You should have 6 double fillets.

Pat the almond paste on the top of each double fillet to form a crust.

Place into the hot oven and bake for 10 minutes. Place under the broiler for 1 minute if you want the crust to be more golden in color.

Meanwhile prepare the salsa: In a medium bowl, toss the mango, strawberries, balsamic vinegar, olive oil, ¼ teaspoon salt, and shallot. Mix together.

Serve the fish with a scoop of salsa and garnish with a sprinkle of mint.

Steamed Thai Sole Rolls

DAIRY OR PARVE ▪ MAKES 6 SERVINGS ▪ NON-GEBROKTS

6 large sole or flounder fillets

coarse sea salt or kosher salt

freshly ground black pepper

1 mango, peeled

1 long red frying pepper

1 (1-inch) piece of fresh ginger, peeled

½ bunch fresh cilantro (discard stems), leaves chopped

1 bunch chives, cut into 2-inch lengths, plus extra for garnish

2 limes, microwaved for 20 seconds

½ cup light cream or nondairy creamer

Another Moshe David delicacy, this dish is colorful and flavorful. Often people see flounder and think the only preparation is to fry it. This is a great healthy alternative to fried flounder.

The cooking method of steaming in plastic wrap concentrates the flavors in the fish as it poaches. This dish can be served hot or made a day in advance, cooled in the plastic and cut and served cold or microwaved the next day.

Place each sole fillet between 2 sheets of plastic wrap and flatten with a meat pounder or the back of a knife. Discard plastic wrap. Trim off uneven ends so that each fillet is rectangular in shape. Season the fish with salt and pepper. Set aside.

Cut ¼-inch slice from either side of the mango pit. Stack the slices, then cut into very thin matchstick-sized pieces.

Cut a 2-inch section from the frying pepper. Slice it in half to open it flat and trim out and discard the seeds and ribs. Cut into very thin matchstick-sized pieces.

Using a mandolin or a vegetable peeler, cut paper-thin slices of ginger. Stack them and then cut into very thin matchstick-sized pieces.

Lay the fish fillets vertically on the work surface. Sprinkle them with an even layer of cilantro. Top with a single horizontal layer of chives, layer of mango, layer of red pepper, and layer of ginger.

Squeeze one of the limes over the fish.

Roll up each fillet, placing them seam-side-down. Roll each fillet tightly in plastic wrap, making the rolls fatter, not longer, by twisting the ends under to form a tight ball.

Place the rolls in a steamer basket. If you don't have one, you can turn a metal strainer upside-down in a large soup pot to form a dome. Bring ½ pot of water to a boil. Place the fish packets on the top of the strainer so they will get steam. Use an upside-down large metal bowl to cover the pot and form a dome to trap the steam. Cook for 15 minutes. You may need to do this in batches, depending on how small the base of the upside-down strainer is.

Place the wrapped fillets into the refrigerator to cool for 15 minutes.

In a small bowl, whisk the cream with the juice of the remaining lime and the zest from half of it. Stir in two chopped cilantro leaves.

Unwrap the fillets. Discard the plastic wrap. Using a sharp knife, cut each into thirds to expose the colors inside. Stand 3 rolls on each plate and drizzle with sauce. Garnish with fresh chives.

Tuna Croquettes

PARVE ▪ MAKES 8 SERVINGS ▪ GEBROKTS

2 (6-ounce) cans solid white tuna in water, drained

⅔ cup unsalted matzo meal

¼ cup mayonnaise

4 large eggs

½ teaspoon garlic powder

½ teaspoon onion powder

½ teaspoon dried minced onion

½ teaspoon fine sea salt

2 tablespoons vegetable oil

On the nights I work, my husband Kal takes over dinner duty. This is one of his famous kid-friendly dishes. Kal claims that over the years he has had many requests from other cookbook authors asking him to share this recipe and until now he has always refused. We should really appreciate his generosity in handing over this keeper.

In a medium-sized bowl, mix the tuna with the matzo meal, mayonnaise, eggs, garlic powder, onion powder, minced onion, and salt. Form 8 patties.

Heat the vegetable oil in a large skillet. When the oil is hot, place the patties into the pan in a single layer, working in batches if necessary, and fry for 3–4 minutes per side until golden-brown.

Remove to plates or a platter.

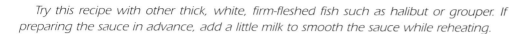

Roasted Lemon-Pepper Cod

DAIRY ▪ MAKES 6 SERVINGS ▪ NON-GEBROKTS

Try this recipe with other thick, white, firm-fleshed fish such as halibut or grouper. If preparing the sauce in advance, add a little milk to smooth the sauce while reheating.

Preheat oven to 375°F.

Line a jelly-roll pan with parchment paper.

Season both sides of each cod fillet with salt. Place them onto prepared pan.

Using a microplane, zest the lemons over the fish, reserving the lemons. Sprinkle with black pepper. Roast for 20 minutes.

Meanwhile, pour the cream into a medium pot. Heat over medium heat until the cream starts to form bubbles around the edges. Reduce the heat to medium-low. Add the juice from the lemons and the onion powder. Simmer over low heat for 7–10 minutes to reduce in volume and until slightly thickened.

Remove the pot from the heat and whisk in the sour cream and any fish juices from the pan. Transfer the fish to plates or a platter. Spoon the sauce over the fish.

6 (6-ounce) cod fillets

fine sea salt

2 lemons

cracked black pepper, or coarsely ground black pepper

2 cups heavy cream

1 teaspoon onion powder

¼ cup sour cream

Potato-Crusted Snapper with Mushroom Sauce

DAIRY ▪ MAKES 6 SERVINGS ▪ NON-GEBROKTS

6 (6-ounce) red snapper fillets, with skin

fine sea salt

freshly ground black pepper

2 cups mashed potato flakes

MUSHROOM SAUCE:

3 tablespoons olive oil, divided

3 tablespoons butter, divided

1 shallot, thinly sliced

3 cloves fresh garlic, chopped

8 ounces assorted exotic mushrooms, such as oyster, shiitake caps, and crimini mushrooms, sliced

2 cups Pinot Grigio or other white wine

½ cup light cream

This dish is always a hit at our table, even with my kids. Red snapper is a mild-tasting fish that, since it doesn't fall apart easily, is a breeze to cook. The potato crust is fabulous and could not be easier. The sauce just puts it over the top.

Season the snapper fillets with salt and pepper. Pour the mashed potato flakes into a plate. Dip the fish into the flakes, pressing to get them to stick. Turn the fillets over and press the flakes into the skin side. Set fish aside.

Meanwhile, prepare the sauce: In a medium skillet, heat 1 tablespoon each of olive oil and butter over medium heat. Add the shallot and garlic; sauté for 4 minutes, or until shiny and translucent.

Add the mushrooms and cook for 2 minutes or until fragrant. Add the wine and bring to a simmer. Allow the wine to reduce for 6–7 minutes. Stir in the light cream. Keep warm.

Cook the fish: In a large skillet, heat 1 tablespoon each of the oil and butter. When the butter is melted and the oil is hot, add 2 or 3 pieces of fish, skin-side-up, in a single layer. Cook for 4–5 minutes or until the potatoes are golden-brown and crusted onto the fish. Flip and cook on the other side for 5 minutes, or until cooked through.

Remove the fish to a platter. Wipe out the pan between batches. Add remaining tablespoon each of olive oil and butter to the pan. When hot, add the remaining snapper fillets. Cook as directed above.

Serve the fish with sauce.

Blackened Tilapia or Red Snapper

DAIRY ▪ MAKES 4 SERVINGS ▪ NON-GEBROKTS

nonstick cooking spray

2 teaspoons onion powder

2 teaspoons garlic powder

1½ teaspoons cayenne pepper

1 teaspoon ground white pepper

1 teaspoon freshly ground black pepper

1 teaspoon paprika

1 teaspoon dried thyme

1 teaspoon dried oregano

1 teaspoon dried basil

1 cup butter, melted

4 (6-ounce) tilapia or red snapper fillets

4 medium fresh tomatoes, each cut in half, tops trimmed so they sit flat

oregano

sour cream

This dish is an authentic Cajun, mouth-on-fire delicacy. Blackened refers to the spices, not the lack of cooking prowess. If you are worried about the heat, coat only one side of the fish with the spice mixture, although it will still be hot. I like to make up a big batch of the spices and keep them in a baby-food jar so that dinner preparation on this dish (it's also great on thinly pounded chicken breasts) is a snap. If you have a cast-iron skillet, it is the way to go. If not, use a nonstick frying pan and get it very hot. Warn your guests, pour a big pitcher of ice water, and enjoy!

Spray a large frying pan or well-seasoned cast-iron skillet with nonstick cooking spray. In a flat plate combine the onion powder, garlic powder, cayenne, white pepper, black pepper, paprika, thyme, oregano, and basil. Mix well.

Dredge each fillet in the melted butter, then coat with the spice mixture on one or both sides. Reserve the melted butter.

If using a cast-iron skillet, get it white-hot. If not, heat the frying pan over medium-high heat until very hot but not smoking.

Carefully place the fillets in the skillet and sear about 3–5 minutes or until blackened. Pour 1 tablespoon of reserved melted butter onto each fillet. Flip the fish over, pour 1 tablespoon of melted butter over each fillet and blacken the other side, about 2–3 minutes. If you spiced only one side, then the second side won't become black; just cook the fish through until it is done. Remove fish to dinner plates.

Brush the tomato halves with the melted butter and sprinkle with oregano. Sear the tomatoes in the frying pan about 3 minutes or until soft. Flip to the other side and cook 1–2 minutes longer.

Serve each fillet with a big dollop of sour cream and two tomato halves.

Parmesan-Crusted Grouper

DAIRY ▪ MAKES 4 SERVINGS ▪ NON-GEBROKTS

Preheat broiler to high. In a small bowl, combine the Parmesan, butter, mayonnaise, and scallions. Set aside.

Place the grouper fillets onto a lightly greased broiler pan. Squeeze the juice from 1 lemon over the fillets and sprinkle with black pepper.

Broil 6 inches from heat for 10 minutes. Remove from oven. Spread the tops of the fillets with cheese mixture.

Return to oven and broil for 2 minutes longer or until the topping is lightly browned and bubbly. Remove fillets to platter.

½ cup grated Parmesan cheese

⅓ cup butter, softened, not melted

2 tablespoons mayonnaise

2 scallions, thinly sliced

2 large or 4 small (1-inch-thick) grouper fillets

1 lemon

freshly ground black pepper

Tuna with Pico de Gallo Sauce

PARVE ▪ MAKES 4 SERVINGS ▪ NON-GEBROKTS

PICO DE GALLO SAUCE:

- 4 plum tomatoes, seeded, cut into ½-inch dice
- ¼ cup cilantro leaves, finely chopped
- 1 lime, divided
- 1 small red onion, minced
- 1 clove fresh garlic, minced
- 1 tablespoon minced, seeded, jalapeño chili pepper (optional)

fine sea salt

freshly ground black pepper

- 4 (6-ounce) tuna fillets

olive oil

Pico de Gallo is a Mexican relish similar to a salsa. Make some extra and serve with steak, hamburgers, or eggs. You can even just serve it with chips for a great snack.

Store parsley and cilantro whole, tightly wrapped, in slightly damp paper towels in the refrigerator. Shave the leaves right before using. To easily shave the leaves from parsley or cilantro stems, scrape the stems with a sharp blade.

Prepare the Pico de Gallo Sauce: In a medium bowl, toss the tomatoes, cilantro, juice of ½ the lime, onion, garlic, and chili pepper if using. Season with salt and pepper. Let the mixture marinate at room temperature for at least 15 minutes.

Prepare the tuna: Rub the tuna on all sides with olive oil, salt, and pepper.

Heat 1 tablespoon olive oil in a medium skillet set over medium heat. When the oil is hot, add the fish, searing 2 minutes per side for medium-rare, 3 minutes per side for medium-well.

Drain the liquid from the Pico de Gallo.

Serve the tuna with a spoonful of the Pico de Gallo. Finish each plate with a small squeeze of the remaining lime half.

Spinach-Cheese Frittata

DAIRY ▪ MAKES 6 SERVINGS ▪ NON-GEBROKTS

This Italian-style omelet bursts with flavor. It's delicious at any temperature, so there is no need to serve it right out of the oven. Try serving at a dairy lunch or late breakfast.

Preheat oven to 400°F.

In a nonstick 10-inch skillet with oven-safe handle (or with handle wrapped in double thickness of foil for baking in the oven later), heat oil over medium heat until hot. Add the scallions and cook about 2 minutes or until softened. Add the spinach and cook about 10 minutes, stirring until moisture has evaporated.

In a large bowl, whisk together the eggs, Swiss or Muenster cheese, basil, garlic, thyme, salt, pepper, and 1 tablespoon Parmesan. Stir the spinach mixture into the egg mixture.

In the skillet, melt the butter over medium heat. Add the spinach/egg mixture back into the skillet and cook for 1 minute, stirring once. Reduce heat to low and cook 5 minutes longer. Mixture will begin to set around the edges. Sprinkle with remaining 1 tablespoon Parmesan. Place skillet into the preheated oven and bake for 10 minutes, or until fritatta sets. Loosen edges of frittata by running a knife along the inside perimeter of the skillet and slide onto a platter.

2 teaspoons olive oil

1 bunch scallions, thinly sliced

10 ounces frozen chopped spinach, thawed and squeezed dry

8 large eggs

1 cup shredded Swiss or Muenster cheese

½ cup fresh basil leaves, chopped

1 clove fresh garlic, minced

½ teaspoon dried thyme

¼ teaspoon fine sea salt

¼ teaspoon freshly ground black pepper

2 tablespoons grated Parmesan cheese, divided

1 tablespoon butter

Baked Farmer Cheese Loaf

DAIRY ▪ MAKES 6-8 SERVINGS ▪ GEBROKTS

This beautiful cheese loaf offers the sweet taste of blintzes without any of the work. The recipe is great as a dairy side dish or served solo.

Preheat oven to 325°F.

In the bowl of an electric mixer, beat the eggs until light and fluffy. Add the sugar, vanilla, and lemon juice. Mix in the farmer cheese.

Line a loaf pan with foil or parchment paper, leaving foil or paper hanging over all four sides. Break the matzo in half and place in a double layer in the bottom of the pan. Pour the cheese mixture over the matzo. Sprinkle with cinnamon/sugar.

Bake, uncovered, for 40–50 minutes or until set in center. Remove from oven. Let cool in pan. Using the foil or parchment, lift the loaf out of the pan and transfer it to your serving platter. Slice and serve.

4 large eggs

1 cup sugar

1 teaspoon vanilla

1 teaspoon fresh lemon juice

16 ounces farmer cheese

1 whole matzo board

cinnamon/sugar

Matzo Brei

6 whole matzo boards

5 large eggs

2 tablespoons milk

¼ teaspoon coarse sea salt
or kosher salt

¼ teaspoon freshly ground
black pepper

2 tablespoons butter

confectioner's sugar

raspberry jelly

In my family, matzo brei is the ultimate bonding food for my husband Kal and my Mom. They spend days planning on when during the holiday they are going to make their batch. Then, they go over the procedure, reminding each other how they do it. Finally, the actual event of making it is followed by hours of review and retrospect about how fabulous it truly was.

Every family has its own tweaked version. Some make it savory by adding in grated onion, mushrooms, and fresh herbs. Even on the sweet end, there are differences, like the addition of cinnamon or serving with syrup vs. confectioner's sugar. However you choose, enjoy and realize you are part of a culinary experience dating back generations.

Break the matzo into 2-inch pieces. Place into a large bowl. Pour very hot water over the matzo and allow it to soak for 1 minute. Drain very well in a colander, pressing out the water. Return the matzo to the bowl.

In a separate bowl, whisk the eggs, milk, salt, and pepper. Pour over the drained matzo.

Melt the butter in a large nonstick skillet over medium heat. Add the matzo-egg mixture and fry until golden brown, about 3 minutes on the first side, 2 minutes on the second side. You can either try to flip it over in one piece by using a plate to turn it out and return it to brown on the other side, or cut it into pieces, and fry in separate parts.

Sprinkle with confectioner's sugar and serve with jelly. You can also serve it with pancake syrup, applesauce, or ketchup.

Popovers

DAIRY OR PARVE ▪ MAKES 8 LARGE POPOVERS ▪ GEBROKTS

nonstick cooking spray

1 cup water

⅓ cup unsalted butter or margarine

½ cup matzo meal

½ cup matzo cake meal

½ teaspoon fine sea salt

2 tablespoons sugar

6 large eggs

Serve these huge and light popovers fresh out of the oven. They are wonderful slathered in butter, honey, or jam for breakfast. You can also set them out in a basket on the table for other meals. For extra-large popovers, bake the batter in greased oven-proof ramekins. For smaller ones use a 12-cup mini (2¼- by 2-inch) popover tin.

Preheat oven to 450°F.

Generously grease the top and inside cups of a nonstick popover tin with nonstick cooking spray.

In a medium pot, bring the water and butter or margarine to a boil over medium heat. Add the matzo meal, matzo cake meal, salt, and sugar. Continue cooking, stirring until the batter no longer sticks to the sides of the pot.

Remove the pot from the stove and transfer the dough to the bowl of an electric mixer. Beat the batter at a high speed for 1 minute. Add eggs one at a time; continue beating after each addition. Beat for another 1–2 minutes, scraping down the sides of the bowl. Transfer the batter to a large measuring cup for easy pouring.

Divide the batter among the 8 or 12 popover compartments. Bake for 20 minutes. Without opening the oven door, reduce heat to 325°F and bake for an additional 30 minutes, or until puffed and golden. Remove from pan and serve.

Blintz Soufflé

12 frozen blintzes, slightly
    defrosted
 6 large eggs
 4 tablespoons butter, melted
1½ cups sour cream
¼ cup orange juice
½ cup sugar
 2 teaspoons vanilla
¼ teaspoon salt
   cinnamon/sugar

One of my favorite out-of-the-box meals on Passover is blintzes. My girlfriends, Estee and Atara, each separately gave me this recipe, which had been in their families for years. It brought back many memories for me as it was a staple at bridal showers the year I got married. I had never thought of using it for Passover. But since the Passover blintzes are so wonderful it makes perfect sense.

The Tuv Taam brand in particular makes the most incredible cheese blintzes and blueberry cheese blintzes. I use an assortment of boxes for this recipe, usually 2 boxes of cheese and one of the fruit variety. Defrost them enough so they separate without breaking, about 15 minutes. A big green salad on the side and my family is in heaven.

Frozen blintzes are available in both gebrokts and non-gebrokts formulations. Check the ingredient panel to see if matzo meal (gebrokts) or potato starch (non-gebrokts) is used.

Preheat oven to 350°F.

Lightly grease a pretty 9- by 13-inch oven-to-table baking dish. Arrange the blintzes in a single layer, overlapping slightly as necessary to fit.

In a large bowl, whisk the eggs, butter, sour cream, orange juice, sugar, vanilla, and salt until it is a smooth batter. Pour over the blintzes. Sprinkle with the cinnamon/sugar.

Bake, uncovered, for 45–55 minutes, until puffed and golden.

Zucchini Casserole

DAIRY ▪ MAKES 10 SERVINGS ▪ GEBROKTS

butter

3 cups thinly sliced, unpeeled zucchini

2 cups shredded mozzarella cheese

1 small onion, chopped

1 cup dry Passover pancake mix

2 tablespoons Parmesan cheese

4 large eggs, lightly beaten

½ cup vegetable oil

½ teaspoon fine sea salt

½ teaspoon dried oregano

freshly ground black pepper

This crustless zucchini pie can be thrown together in minutes. It is a crowd-pleaser and goes nicely as a side for fish.

Preheat oven to 350°F.

Lightly grease a 13- by 9-inch baking dish with butter.

Combine zucchini, mozzarella cheese, onion, pancake mix, Parmesan cheese, eggs, oil, salt, oregano, and pepper in a large bowl, mixing well with a large spoon. Spoon into the prepared dish. Bake 40 minutes or until golden brown.

Spinach-Cheese Lasagne

DAIRY ▪ MAKES 10-12 SERVINGS ▪ GEBROKTS

1 (10-ounce) package frozen chopped spinach, defrosted and squeezed dry

1 pound ricotta or cottage cheese

1 large egg

½ teaspoon dried oregano

freshly ground black pepper

3 (7-ounce) bags shredded mozzarella, divided

1 (26-ounce) jar marinara sauce

9 whole matzo boards

1 cup water

So simple yet so delicious, this dish is perfect when you have no time to fuss in the kitchen.

Preheat oven to 350°F.

In a large mixing bowl, combine the spinach, ricotta or cottage cheese, egg, oregano, pepper, and ½ the mozzarella.

Grease a 9- by 13-inch shallow pan. Ladle a thin layer of sauce into the bottom of the pan. Layer 3 matzo boards (breaking to fit), ½ the cheese mixture, and a layer of sauce. Top with 3 more matzos, the remaining cheese mixture, and a layer of sauce. Add 3 more matzos and a layer of sauce. Top with the remaining mozzarella. Pour water around the sides. Cover and bake for 45 minutes; uncover and bake 30–40 minutes longer. Cheese will be melted and bubbly.

SIDE DISHES

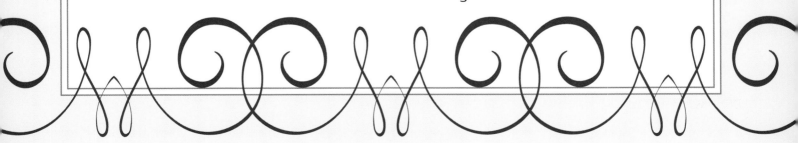

Matzo Primavera

MEAT OR PARVE ▪ MAKES 9 SERVINGS ▪ GEBROKTS

nonstick cooking spray

3 matzo boards

1 cup vegetable or chicken stock

¼ cup plus 2 tablespoons olive oil, divided

6 fresh basil leaves, minced

2 cloves fresh garlic, minced

¼ teaspoon fine sea salt

¼ teaspoon freshly ground black pepper

2 zucchini, unpeeled, sliced into ¼-inch rounds

2 yellow squash, unpeeled, sliced into ¼-inch rounds

2-3 Asian or Japanese eggplant, unpeeled, sliced into ¼-inch rounds

5-6 plum or Roma tomatoes, sliced into ¼-inch rounds

¾ teaspoon parve chicken or vegetable consommé powder, divided

finely chopped fresh basil, for garnish

The perfectly seared vegetables peek out from between the matzos, making a lovely presentation.

Preheat oven to 350°F.

Spray a 9- by 9-inch baking pan with nonstick cooking spray. Set aside.

Place the matzo boards in 1–2 jelly-roll or other shallow pans large enough to hold them in a single layer. Pour stock over the matzos just to cover, and allow to stand for 7–8 minutes, until pliable but not mushy.

Meanwhile, pour ¼ cup olive oil into another jelly-roll pan. Add the basil, garlic, salt, and pepper. Place the sliced zucchini, squash, eggplant, and tomato slices into the oil mixture. Turn each piece to coat.

Heat the remaining olive oil in a large skillet over medium heat. Sear the zucchini, squash, and eggplant in a single layer, turning as each piece softens and turns golden.

Remove from pan. Add the tomatoes, cooking for 1 minute per side until softened but not mushy. Remove from pan.

In the prepared pan, arrange a single layer of overlapping zucchini. Lay 1 matzo on top of it. Sprinkle with ¼ teaspoon consommé powder. Top with a single layer of overlapping squash slices. Layer a second matzo board. Sprinkle a ¼ teaspoon consommé powder. Top with a layer of overlapping eggplant, followed by the third matzo, sprinkling of ¼ teaspoon consommé powder, and a final layer of overlapping tomatoes.

Bake, uncovered for 20 minutes. Garnish with chopped basil arranged in narrow rows.

Mushroom Mashed Potatoes

DAIRY OR PARVE ▪ MAKES 6 SERVINGS ▪ NON-GEBROKTS

2½ pounds Yukon Gold or
    russet potatoes, peeled
    and cut into 1-inch chunks

fine sea salt

3 tablespoons vegetable oil

5 shallots, thinly sliced

1 small onion, chopped

3.5 ounces shiitake
    mushrooms, cut into ½-
    inch dice, stems discarded

3.5 ounces crimini mushrooms,
    cut into ½-inch dice

4 tablespoons butter or
    margarine

Mashed potatoes can be prepared 2 hours ahead. Cover and keep at room temperature. Rewarm over low heat, stirring frequently. Never use a food processor to mash potatoes, as it destroys the starch granules and turns them to paste. If you must make them more in advance, cover tightly with foil and heat in a 325°F oven for 1½ hours, to thoroughly reheat.

Yukon Gold potatoes will yield a creamier result, while russet potatoes will give you a fluffier one.

Place the potatoes into a large pot. Cover with water. Sprinkle in 2 teaspoons salt. Bring to a boil. Cook for 30–35 minutes, until potatoes are fork-tender.

Meanwhile, heat the oil in a medium skillet. Add the shallots, onion, and mushrooms. Turn the heat to medium-low and sauté for 25–30 minutes, stirring with a wooden spoon every few minutes to make sure the shallots are not sticking to the pan. The mushrooms will be nicely browned.

When potatoes are soft, drain. Mash with a hand masher, potato ricer, or electric mixer until fluffy and smooth. Immediately add the butter or margarine so it melts into the potatoes. Season with salt and black pepper to taste. Add the mushroom-shallot mixture with the oil in which they cooked. Serve warm.

Acorn Squash with Frosted Cranberries

PARVE ▪ MAKES 8 SERVINGS ▪ NON-GEBROKTS

Acorn squash, like all winter squash, can be dangerous to cut. I ask the workers in the produce department at the supermarket to cut them in half and wrap them in plastic wrap. If you can find only large acorn squash, just cut the squash in half. After they are softened by cooking, you can cut each half in half again for more manageable servings.

Preheat oven to 375°F.

Place the acorn squash cut-side-down into a baking pan. Pour ½ inch of water around the squash. Bake 45 minutes.

In a saucepan, bring the water and sugar to a boil over medium-high heat. When sugar dissolves, reduce heat and add the cranberries. Simmer for 15 minutes. Drain off liquid. Remove the berries to a sheet of waxed paper. Separate with a fork. Set aside.

Remove squash from oven and pour off the water from the pan. Turn the squash cut-side-up. In a small bowl, mix the brown sugar, honey, ginger, cinnamon, margarine, salt, and pepper. Divide mixture evenly among the squash halves. Return to the oven for another 30–35 minutes, basting with sauce, until squash is soft.

Toss the cranberries with a little sugar to coat them. Remove the squash to a platter and fill each cavity with frosted cranberries.

ACORN SQUASH:

4 small acorn squash, cut in half around the "waist," seeded

4 tablespoons dark brown sugar

4 tablespoons honey

pinch of ground ginger

¼ teaspoon cinnamon

4 tablespoons margarine, at room temperature

fine sea salt

freshly ground black pepper

FROSTED CRANBERRIES:

1 cup water

1 cup sugar, plus extra for frosting

2 cups fresh or frozen cranberries, unthawed

Cherry Tomato Crisp

PARVE ▪ MAKES 6 SERVINGS ▪ GEBROKTS

6 tablespoons olive oil, divided

2 pints cherry tomatoes, stems removed

½ cup matzo meal

2 tablespoons chopped fresh parsley

1 tablespoon dried minced onion

2 cloves fresh garlic, minced

½ teaspoon fine sea salt

½ teaspoon freshly ground black pepper

If you think of crisps as being made only of tree-fruit, think again! Cherry tomatoes are amazing and work great too.

Preheat oven to 425°F.

Lightly coat a shallow oven-to-table baking dish with 2 tablespoons olive oil. Toss the tomatoes in the oil to coat. Arrange in a single layer in the dish. In a medium bowl, combine the matzo meal, parsley, minced onion, minced garlic, salt, pepper, and 4 remaining tablespoons oil. Mix well. Sprinkle over the tomatoes.

Roast for 20–25 minutes, until crumbs are golden-brown and tomatoes are tender. Serve hot.

Crispy Cauliflower

PARVE ▪ MAKES 4-6 SERVINGS ▪ GEBROKTS

Preheat oven to 375°F.

Line a cookie sheet with parchment paper. Set aside.

In a medium bowl mix the matzo meal with the garlic powder, salt, lemon juice, basil, pepper, and scallions.

Cut the cauliflower florets into bite-sized pieces and place them into a large mixing bowl. Discard the hard center of the cauliflower.

Add the oil to the bowl. Toss to coat the florets.

Lightly beat the eggs in a small mixing bowl. Add the eggs to the cauliflower and toss to coat. Add the flavored matzo meal. Shake to coat the cauliflower.

Place the cauliflower onto the prepared cookie sheet in a single layer. Place the cookie sheet into the oven and bake for 35 minutes, until golden.

½ cup matzo meal
½ teaspoon garlic powder
½ teaspoon fine sea salt
1 teaspoon lemon juice
½ teaspoon dried basil
½ teaspoon black pepper
2 small scallions, minced
1 head cauliflower
2 tablespoons olive oil
2 large eggs

Hasselback Potatoes

PARVE ▪ MAKES 8 SERVINGS ▪ NON-GEBROKTS

8 small Idaho baking potatoes or Yukon Gold potatoes

8 cloves fresh garlic, sliced into thin slivers

coarse sea salt or kosher salt

coarse black pepper

olive oil

My friend Jill Raff was the stylist on the original Kosher by Design. She shared this recipe concept with me. It is an old family favorite technique for dressing up a plain baked potato.

This is a neat trick for cutting the potatoes so that you cut even slices but don't cut through to the bottom. Place the potato into a wooden spoon. The sides of the spoon will keep you from cutting through. For bigger potatoes, like Idaho potatoes, place a chopstick or wooden spoon along each of the two long sides. With one hand holding the potato and chopsticks or spoons in place, slice the potato widthwise. The knife should touch the chopsticks or handles of the spoons at every slice, leaving the slices attached at the bottom of the potato. This will serve as a guide to keep your slices even and keep you from slicing through as well.

Preheat oven to 450°F.

Using a sharp or electric knife, starting at one end and going to the other end, cut slits into the top of each potato ⅛ of an inch apart, being careful not to cut all the way to the bottom of the potato; see methods above. Place the potatoes on a baking sheet.

Place a garlic sliver into each slit. Sprinkle each potato with salt and pepper. Drizzle with olive oil.

Bake 1 hour, baste with the pan oil, and then continue to bake for another 15 minutes, until potatoes are soft.

Zucchini-Tomato Gratin

PARVE ▪ MAKES 8-10 SERVINGS ▪ GEBROKTS

4 tablespoons (½ stick) margarine, divided

3 tablespoons olive oil, divided

1½ pounds zucchini (about 3 medium), peeled and thinly sliced

1 medium onion, finely chopped

1 clove fresh garlic, chopped

4 medium round tomatoes, coarsely chopped

fine sea salt

freshly ground black pepper

½ cup matzo meal

This dish is garden fresh. For dairy meals, melt some shredded mozzarella over the top.

Preheat oven to 400°F.

Lightly grease a shallow oven-proof dish. Set aside.

In a large skillet or saucepan, heat 2 tablespoons of the margarine and 1 tablespoon of the oil over medium heat. Add the zucchini. Cover and cook 5–6 minutes or until tender; set aside.

In a medium skillet, warm the remaining 2 tablespoons olive oil over moderate heat. Add the onion and cook for 5 minutes. Add the garlic and continue cooking for 1 minute longer. Reduce the heat and add the tomatoes. Cover and cook for 15 minutes. Season well with salt and pepper. Pour off some liquid.

Stir the zucchini into the tomatoes. Pour evenly into the prepared dish. Sprinkle with matzo meal and dot with remaining 2 tablespoons of margarine. Bake uncovered for 25–30 minutes or until top is golden and crisp.

Meichel

MEAT ▪ MAKES 8-10 SERVINGS ▪ GEBROKTS

1 (1-pound) box matzo farfel

1 tablespoon vegetable oil

1 tablespoon margarine

1 large onion, finely chopped

1 (10-ounce) box sliced mushrooms

1 (10-ounce) can condensed chicken soup, undiluted

fine sea salt

freshly ground black pepper

This was a signature Passover dish of my mother-in-law, Myrna. We all looked forward to it every year. Years ago, as a Pesach present I bought her a huge, 14-inch frying pan. Not that I was trying to drop any hints, but my family was thrilled with the extra-large batch of meichel that it turned out.

Place the matzo farfel into a large bowl. Cover with boiling water and let soften for 2–3 minutes. Do not let it sit any longer or the end result will be mushy. Drain the water; set aside.

In a large skillet, heat the oil and margarine over medium heat. Add the onion and sauté for 6–8 minutes or until it begins to turn golden. Add the mushrooms and sauté 3–4 minutes longer.

Add the drained matzo farfel to the skillet and sauté. Slowly add the chicken soup, using as little or as much as you need to reach the consistency of a pilaf. Season with salt and pepper.

Cauliflower "Popcorn"

PARVE ▪ MAKES 8 SERVINGS ▪ NON-GEBROKTS

You will pop these gorgeous golden carb-friendly treats into your mouth like popcorn. The simple high-heat roasting method brings out the natural sugars of the vegetable and the spice combination works great in both flavor and color. Don't cut florets too small because they shrivel while cooking.

Preheat oven to 450°F.

Line a jelly-roll pan or baking sheet with parchment paper.

In a large bowl, combine the salt, sugar, onion powder, garlic powder, paprika, turmeric, and oil. Add cauliflower florets and toss to evenly coat.

Place in a single layer onto the prepared sheet.

Roast, uncovered, for 30–35 minutes, until the largest pieces can be pierced with a fork. If the tops are starting to get too brown, toss the cauliflower during the baking process.

2 heads cauliflower, cut into medium-sized florets, stems discarded

1 teaspoon fine sea salt

2 teaspoons sugar

¼ teaspoon onion powder

¼ teaspoon garlic powder

½ teaspoon paprika

¼-½ teaspoon ground turmeric

6-8 tablespoons olive oil

Oranges Stuffed with Cranberry-Cherry Relish

PARVE • MAKES 10-12 SERVINGS • NON-GEBROKTS

2 cups firmly packed dark brown sugar

1½ cups golden raisins

1 orange, unpeeled, quartered, seeded, cut into ¼-inch dice

1 lemon, unpeeled, quartered, seeded, cut into ¼-inch dice

1 cup canned pitted sweet dark cherries, drained

½ cup white vinegar

1 cinnamon stick

½ teaspoon ground cinnamon

½ teaspoon ground nutmeg

½ teaspoon ground cloves

1½ cups fresh cranberries

½ cup chopped walnuts

small navel oranges, for optional garnish

cinnamon sticks, for optional garnish

When my brother got married, not only did I get Jessica, a sister-in-law whom I adore, but the bonus was that she brought along some great family recipes. This is one of them.

In a large pot, combine the brown sugar, raisins, orange, lemon, cherries, vinegar, cinnamon stick, ground cinnamon, nutmeg, and cloves. Bring to a boil over medium heat, stirring frequently. Reduce heat and simmer for 10 minutes. Add the cranberries and simmer until they begin to pop, about 15 minutes longer. Remove cinnamon stick. Cover and refrigerate until cold. Can be made in advance. When ready to serve, mix in the walnuts.

You can serve the relish in a pretty bowl, or halve and hollow out small navel oranges. Stuff each with a mound of relish and stick a cinnamon stick in each.

Tzimmes Soufflé

PARVE ▪ MAKES 10-12 SERVINGS ▪ GEBROKTS

This recipe is great all year-round. For an extra-special presentation, make this recipe in individual ramekins for single servings as pictured below.

Preheat oven to 350°F.

Spray a 9- by 9-inch square pan with nonstick cooking spray. Set aside.

In a small bowl, lightly beat the egg yolks. Set aside.

In a large bowl, beat the egg whites until stiff. Using a spatula, fold in the carrots, sugar, and matzo meal. Fold in the egg yolks, oil, lemon juice, orange juice, and pineapple with the syrup.

Pour into the prepared baking dish. Bake 40–45 minutes or until top is golden. Scoop or spoon out.

nonstick cooking spray

5 large eggs, separated

2 cups finely grated carrots, about 5-6 large carrots

1 cup sugar

¾ cup matzo meal

½ cup vegetable oil

1 teaspoon lemon juice

2 tablespoons orange juice

1 (20-ounce) can crushed pineapple with heavy syrup

Fanned Eggplant with Orange Kumquats

MEAT OR PARVE ▪ MAKES 6 SERVINGS ▪ NON-GEBROKTS

ORANGE KUMQUATS:

1 cup sugar

1 cup water

1 1-inch chunk fresh ginger, peeled

2 sprigs fresh rosemary

½ medium orange

1 bay leaf

1 stick cinnamon

1 cup kumquats, ends trimmed off each

DUCK SAUCE GLAZE:

1 tablespoon vegetable oil

2 cloves fresh garlic, minced

2 teaspoons fresh minced ginger

½ cup duck sauce

1 teaspoon parve chicken consommé powder

2 tablespoons chicken or vegetable stock

FANNED EGGPLANTS:

3 small Italian eggplants, each cut in half lengthwise

olive oil

fine sea salt

freshly ground black pepper

parve chicken consommé powder

Kumquats have been called "the little gold gems of the citrus family." They are the only citrus fruit that can be eaten skin and all. They are bitter but after being candied in this recipe, they are a real gourmet delight.

Preheat oven to 375°F.

Cover a large cookie sheet with parchment paper. Set aside.

In a medium pot, bring the sugar and water to a simmer over medium heat. Add the ginger, rosemary, orange half, bay leaf, cinnamon, and kumquats. Simmer for 15 minutes. Turn off the heat and allow to stand.

In a small pot, heat the vegetable oil. Add the minced garlic and ginger. Sauté until fragrant, about 1 minute. Add the duck sauce, consommé powder, and stock. Stir. Set aside.

Place an eggplant half, cut-side-down, on a cutting board. A little on the bias, cut ¼-inch slices so that the eggplant remains attached at the stem. Press with the palm of your hand to flatten and fan out. Repeat with remaining eggplants. Completely brush the fanned eggplants on both sides with olive oil. Season both sides with salt, pepper, and consommé powder.

In a large skillet, pan-sear the eggplants, pressing them down so that most of the slices make contact with the pan. Cook until golden-brown and soft. Do this in batches if necessary. Place on prepared cookie sheet.

Brush the eggplants with the duck sauce glaze. Bake for 10 minutes until shiny and soft.

Remove the kumquats from their liquid, discarding everything else in the pot. Coarsely chop them and sprinkle on the fanned eggplants.

Two-Tone Potatoes with Pesto Sauce

PARVE ▪ MAKES 8 SERVINGS ▪ NON-GEBROKTS

1 cup fresh basil leaves

2 large shallots

4 cloves fresh garlic

2 tablespoons pine nuts

⅓ cup olive oil, plus more for drizzling

1½ pounds small red new potatoes, unpeeled

1½ pounds small white round potatoes, unpeeled

coarse sea salt or kosher salt

freshly ground black pepper

Preheat oven to 400°F.

In the bowl of a food processor fitted with a metal blade, process the basil, shallots, garlic, and pine nuts until finely chopped. Drizzle in the olive oil. Pulse to combine into a smooth paste.

Place the potatoes in a large baking dish. Drizzle with olive oil. Season generously with salt and pepper. Roast, uncovered, for 40 minutes.

Pour the pesto over the potatoes; toss to coat. Continue roasting until potatoes are fork tender and golden brown, about 25–30 minutes longer.

Roasted-Garlic Asparagus

PARVE ▪ MAKES 6 SERVINGS ▪ NON-GEBROKTS

Simple, elegant, healthy. What more could you want from a side dish? For a prettier presentation, you can trim the "thorns" from the asparagus with a vegetable peeler.

Preheat oven to 400°F.

Line a large jelly-roll pan with parchment paper. Set aside.

In a small pot, heat the oil, garlic, onion powder, and parsley on medium-low heat. Cook for 3 minutes, until the garlic mixture is fragrant but not browned.

Spread the asparagus in a single layer on the prepared pan. Lightly sprinkle with coarse sea salt and freshly ground pepper. Drizzle on the garlic-oil mixture.

Roast for 8–10 minutes, until the asparagus are bright green; do not overcook.

Transfer to a platter and serve hot.

½ cup extra-virgin olive oil

8 cloves fresh garlic, minced

1 teaspoon onion powder

2 tablespoons fresh finely chopped parsley

2 pounds thin asparagus, ends trimmed

fleur de sel or coarse sea salt

freshly ground black pepper

Quinoa Timbales
with Grapefruit Vinaigrette

PARVE ▪ MAKES 8 SERVINGS ▪ NON-GEBROKTS

1 (20-ounce) box quinoa, rinsed and prepared according to package directions

2 tablespoons margarine

1 small zucchini, cut into ¼-inch dice

1 small carrot, peeled, cut into ¼-inch dice

1 small yellow squash, cut into ¼-inch dice

½ teaspoon garlic powder

¼ teaspoon ground ginger

¼ teaspoon fine sea salt

¼ teaspoon freshly ground black pepper

3-4 cucumbers (each 8-10 inches), unpeeled

olive oil

GRAPEFRUIT VINAIGRETTE:

3 tablespoons juice from a large grapefruit; save segments for garnish

2 tablespoons extra-virgin olive oil

¼ teaspoon fine sea salt

¼ teaspoon freshly ground black pepper

GARNISH:

zucchini, unpeeled

yellow squash, unpeeled

Four-ounce ramekins are the perfect size for this dish. Moshe David, who turns out hundreds of these at any given holiday meal, uses disposable aluminum muffin cups.

A note about quinoa: Although the halachic status of quinoa is ambiguous, many kashrus organizations deem it acceptable, while others do not. Consult your local rabbi for clarification.

While the quinoa is cooking, prepare the vegetables.

In a large skillet, melt the margarine over medium heat. Add the zucchini, carrot, and squash. Sauté until soft, about 4–5 minutes. Season with garlic powder, ginger, salt, and pepper. When the quinoa is cooked, drain and add to vegetables. Toss to mix. Set aside.

Using a hand-held mandolin, cut 32, thin, lengthwise slices of cucumber. Brush 8 ramekins with olive oil. Stand the cucumber slices around the inside perimeter of the ramekin in a double layer to form a surrounding wall. Pack a ½ cup of quinoa into each ramekin. Hold a plate over the top of each ramekin and flip out the timbale.

Prepare the vinaigrette: In a small bowl whisk the grapefruit juice, extra-virgin olive oil, salt, and pepper.

Drizzle vinaigrette over each timbale.

Garnish with grapefruit segments and shapes cut out of the zucchini and squash.

Roasted Caramelized Carrots

PARVE ▪ MAKES 8-10 SERVINGS ▪ NON-GEBROKTS

3 pounds carrots, peeled and sliced into ¼-inch discs

½ cup sugar

3-4 tablespoons vegetable oil

For ease of preparation, you can purchase bags of pre-sliced carrots. They are sold in bias cuts and coins; either is fine and really saves time.

Preheat oven to 400°F.

In a large bowl, combine the carrots, sugar, and oil. Toss to coat. Spread the carrots into two jelly-roll pans in single layers.

Roast about 45 minutes–1 hour on the middle and top racks of the oven until carrots are caramelized and begin to shrivel. Switch the pans midway through cooking time. Shake occasionally to prevent the carrots from burning.

Cranberry-Pineapple Kugel

PARVE ▪ MAKES 12 SERVINGS ▪ GEBROKTS

Preheat oven to 350°F.

Heavily spray a 10-inch springform pan with nonstick cooking spray.

Place the farfel into a large strainer. Wet the farfel under running water and drain.

In a large bowl, mix the farfel, sugar, cinnamon, cranberry sauce, oil, and orange juice. Use a wooden spoon to thoroughly combine. Press into the prepared pan.

Prepare the pineapple topping: In a medium bowl, whisk the eggs and sugar. Add the oil, potato starch, and pineapple. Mix. Pour over the cranberry base.

Bake, uncovered, for 50 minutes. Run a knife or spatula around the perimeter to loosen the kugel before unmolding.

CRANBERRY BASE:
- nonstick cooking spray
- 4 cups matzo farfel
- ⅓ cup sugar
- 1 teaspoon ground cinnamon
- 1 (16-ounce) can whole berry cranberry sauce
- ⅔ cup vegetable oil
- ¼ cup orange juice

PINEAPPLE TOPPING:
- 4 large eggs, lightly beaten
- ½ cup sugar
- ½ cup vegetable oil
- ¼ cup potato starch
- 1 (20-ounce) can crushed pineapple, drained

Stuffed Baked Potatoes

DAIRY ▪ MAKES 3 STUFFED BAKED POTATOES ▪ NON-GEBROKTS

3 large russet potatoes

olive oil

BROCCOLI-CHEDDAR TOPPING:

1 cup broccoli florets

½ cup shredded Cheddar cheese

2 teaspoons potato starch

2 teaspoons milk

½ teaspoon fine sea salt

SALSA-CHEDDAR TOPPING:

¾ cup bottled salsa

⅓ cup shredded Cheddar cheese

**SOUR CREAM
AND CHIVE TOPPING:**

½ cup sour cream

6 chives

Any of these toppings makes enough to fill three potatoes.

Preheat oven to 400°F.

Scrub each potato to make sure it is clean. Dry them.

With a knife, cut a large deep "x" into the top of each potato. Place the potatoes onto a baking sheet. With a pastry brush, brush olive oil all over each potato. Place into the hot oven and bake for 1 hour. When the potatoes are done, carefully remove them from the oven.

With paper towels to protect your fingers, push the ends of the potatoes to the center to open the slits more fully and help fluff the potatoes.

Prepare topping of your choice.

Broccoli-Cheddar Topping: Place the broccoli florets on a cutting board and chop them into ¾-inch pieces. Place the chopped broccoli into a small pot. Add water to cover. Bring to a boil over medium heat. Cook the broccoli until tender, about 5–6 minutes. Drain. Return the broccoli to the pot. Add the cheese.

Place the potato starch into a small bowl. Add the milk and stir to dissolve. Add this potato starch mixture to the pot. Add the salt.

Place the pot over medium heat, stirring with a wooden spoon or silicone spatula until the cheese is melted and smooth. Pour ⅓ into each potato slit; it will overflow down the sides.

Salsa-Cheddar Topping: Place ¼ cup of the salsa into the slit of each potato; it will leak out of the opening. Top each potato with ⅓ of the Cheddar cheese. Return the potatoes to the oven for 5 minutes, until the cheese is melted.

Sour Cream and Chive topping: Place the sour cream into a small bowl.

With a pair of scissors, snip the chives into tiny pieces. Add to the bowl. Stir to combine. Place a large spoonful into the slit of the potato.

Thai Quinoa

PARVE ▪ MAKES 6-8 SERVINGS ▪ NON-GEBROKTS

1½ cups dry quinoa

3 cups water

1 jalapeño pepper, seeded and minced

6 fresh basil leaves, finely chopped

3 sprigs fresh cilantro, leaves gently torn (discard stems)

⅓ cup minced red onion (about ½ small red onion)

½ firm mango, not too ripe, peeled, pitted, and cut into ⅛-inch dice

2 tablespoons extra-virgin olive oil

¾ teaspoon fine sea salt

1 tablespoon plus 1 teaspoon lime juice

Quinoa has become very popular with cooks today, especially during Passover when this berry, which tastes like a grain, stands in nicely for what we crave. It is high in protein and has other healthful characteristics.

A note about quinoa: Although the halachic status of quinoa is ambiguous, many kashrus organizations deem it acceptable, while others do not. Consult your local rabbi for clarification.

Rinse the quinoa thoroughly either in a strainer or in a pot, and drain. (Do not skip this step or a bitter, soap-like natural coating will remain.) Once the quinoa is drained, place it into a medium pot with the water. Bring to a boil. Reduce the heat and simmer until the water is absorbed, about 10–15 minutes, or until the grains turn translucent and the outer layer pops off. Drain.

Meanwhile, in a medium bowl, combine the minced jalapeño, basil, cilantro, red onion, and mango. Drizzle in the oil, salt, and lime juice. Stir to combine.

Add the drained quinoa and toss to combine. Season with salt to taste. Serve warm or at room temperature.

Traditional Potato Kugel

PARVE ▪ MAKES 12-14 SERVINGS ▪ NON-GEBROKTS

My Mom makes the best potato kugel. She lovingly grates each potato by hand. She does this with a full heart, like everything she does for my family. However, hand-grating makes me nervous. Luckily, this recipe captures the taste and flavor of hand-grated potatoes with the ease of a food processor.

Preheat oven to 425°F.

Place the oil into a large 9- by 13-inch rectangular baking pan; set aside.

Fill a large bowl with cold water and add some ice cubes. Peel the potatoes and place them into the bowl of cold water. This will prevent them from turning brown.

Finely chop the onions in the container of a food processor fitted with a metal blade. Remove them to a large bowl. Cut the potatoes into chunks and place them into the food processor; process until almost smooth. Add the potatoes to the onions.

Add the salt, pepper, and sugar to the potato mixture. Add the eggs and stir until thoroughly combined.

Place the baking pan with oil into the oven. When the oil sizzles, carefully remove from oven and spoon some of it into the potato mixture. This will help make the kugel fluffy. Mix well. Pour the potatoes into the oiled pan. Bake, uncovered, for 1 hour.

½ cup vegetable oil

8 medium potatoes

2 medium onions, quartered

1 tablespoon fine sea salt

1 teaspoon freshly ground black pepper

2½ tablespoons sugar

5 large eggs, beaten with a whisk

Cauliflower Française

MEAT OR PARVE ▪ MAKES 6-8 SERVINGS ▪ NON-GEBROKTS

2 heads cauliflower

1 cup plus 1 tablespoon potato starch, divided

fine sea salt

freshly ground black pepper

3 large eggs

olive oil-flavored cooking spray

3 tablespoons margarine

juice of 1 lemon

1 cup white wine

½ cup chicken or vegetable stock

3 tablespoons chopped fresh curly parsley

Française is generally a preparation reserved for chicken or thinly sliced veal. I thought I would try it with cauliflower, one of my favorite vegetables. The results? C'est magnifique!

Preheat oven to 425°F.

Cover 2 large cookie sheets with parchment paper. Set aside.

Trim the cauliflower to the base so that it sits flat on the cutting board. Trim off the two outer ends. Make 3 (¾-inch) lengthwise cuts to yield 3–4 large steaks from each head of cauliflower. Keep the remaining pieces that fall off in flat intact bunches, as much as possible.

In a shallow bowl or pie plate, stir together the 1 cup potato starch, ½ teaspoon salt, and ¼ teaspoon pepper. Dredge the large cauliflower steaks, one at a time, in the potato starch mixture, shaking off the excess. Toss the smaller pieces in the potato starch and shake off excess. Lightly beat eggs in another shallow bowl or pie plate. Dip the cauliflower into the eggs to coat, letting the excess drip off; then place in single layers on prepared cookie sheets.

Once all the cauliflower is battered, spray the tops of the cauliflower steaks and pieces with olive oil-flavored cooking spray. Season with salt and pepper. Place into the hot oven and bake for 20–25 minutes or until the cauliflower is tender.

In a medium skillet, melt the margarine. Whisk in the 1 tablespoon potato starch. Add the juice of the lemon, wine, and stock. Season with ¼ teaspoon salt and ¼ teaspoon pepper. Bring to a simmer and cook for 2 minutes or until thickened and translucent. Stir in the parsley. Taste and re-season as needed. Spoon sauce over the cauliflower.

Spicy Potato Stacks

PARVE ▪ MAKES 6-8 POTATO STACKS ▪ NON-GEBROKTS

1 teaspoon garlic powder

1 teaspoon onion powder

1 teaspoon paprika

½ teaspoon freshly ground black pepper

½ teaspoon fine sea salt

½ teaspoon cayenne pepper

2 large Yukon Gold potatoes, unpeeled, sliced into ½-inch slices, ends discarded

2 large red potatoes, unpeeled, sliced into ½-inch slices, ends discarded

2 sweet potatoes, peeled, sliced into ½-inch slices, ends discarded

½ cup extra-virgin olive oil

fine sea salt

fresh rosemary sprigs

Look for potatoes of similar diameter so that they line up easily when stacked. You should be able to get 3 to 4 slices from the Yukon Gold and red potatoes and 5 to 6 slices from each sweet potato. To make these stacks hot and spicy, add cayenne pepper to the barbecue spice blend. You can also slice an onion into very thin rings, coat with the same spices and roast alongside the potatoes. Insert a roasted onion slice between each potato slice.

Preheat oven to 400°F.

Cover a large jelly-roll pan or cookie sheet with parchment paper. Set aside.

In a small bowl, mix garlic powder, onion powder, paprika, black pepper, salt, and cayenne. Set aside.

Place all the sliced potatoes into a large mixing bowl.

Pour the oil into the bowl. Toss to coat. Sprinkle in the spice blend. Toss to coat well. Arrange the potatoes in a single layer on prepared baking sheet. Roast the potatoes, uncovered, for 20 minutes.

Season with a sprinkle of salt.

Make layered stacks using the three kinds of potatoes. Press a rosemary skewer through the center to secure each stack. Serve hot.

Broccoli and Cauliflower Gratin

DAIRY OR PARVE ▪ MAKES 12 SERVINGS ▪ GEBROKTS

nonstick cooking spray

1 head broccoli,
   cut into small florets

1 head cauliflower,
   cut into small florets

⅔ cup light cream or
   nondairy creamer

½ teaspoon fine sea salt

⅛ teaspoon freshly ground
   black pepper

1 teaspoon vegetable or
   parve chicken consommé
   powder

pinch dried thyme, crushed

pinch white pepper

pinch garlic powder

pinch nutmeg

1 bay leaf

1 tablespoon potato starch

1 cup vegetable or chicken
   stock

3½ tablespoons butter or
   margarine, divided

1 clove fresh garlic, minced

2 cups matzo farfel

¼ cup minced fresh parsley

½ cup grated Parmesan
   cheese, optional for dairy
   meals

1 tablespoon fresh thyme
   leaves

This dish can be prepared in one large casserole dish or for single servings in 4-ounce ramekins.

Preheat oven to 375°F.

Spray a medium oven-to-table round casserole dish with nonstick cooking spray.

Bring a large pot of water to a boil. Add the broccoli and cauliflower and simmer until soft but not mushy.

In a medium pot, whisk the cream or creamer, salt, pepper, consommé powder, thyme, white pepper, garlic powder, and nutmeg. Add the bay leaf. Bring to a simmer over medium heat. Dissolve the potato starch in the stock. Add to the pot. Simmer for 5 minutes. Add ½ tablespoon butter or margarine and stir until melted.

Drain the broccoli and cauliflower and place into the prepared dish. Pour the cream mixture over the vegetables. Stir to coat. Gently tap to bring some of the cream to the bottom.

In a medium skillet over medium heat, melt the remaining 3 tablespoons butter or margarine. Add the garlic. Sauté until translucent about 1 minute. Add the farfel. Season with ⅛ teaspoon salt and ⅛ teaspoon black pepper. Sauté until golden brown and toasted, about 2–3 minutes. Turn off the heat. Mix the parsley, cheese if using and fresh thyme leaves. Stir to combine. Sprinkle this topping over the dish.

Bake, uncovered, for 20 minutes, until cream is bubbly and cheese, if using, is melted.

Glazed Root Vegetables

PARVE ▪ MAKES 10 SERVINGS ▪ NON-GEBROKTS

1 large red beet, peeled and cut into 1-inch chunks

1 large red onion, peeled and cut into 1-inch chunks

2 medium sweet potatoes, peeled and cut into 1-inch cubes

1 cup baby carrots

2 large parsnips, peeled and cut into 1-inch cubes

1 acorn squash, with skin, cut into 2-inch chunks

½ cup orange juice

3 tablespoons duck sauce

1 tablespoon coarse sea salt or kosher salt

¼ teaspoon dried thyme

¼ teaspoon dried rosemary, crumbled

Don't be afraid to turn to your slow cooker for a healthful and tempting side dish. If you don't have a slow cooker for Passover, just roast uncovered for 1½ hours at 375°F. This recipe yields a bounty of gorgeous root vegetables. The beet tinges everything a light pink. This dish will certainly please the vegetarians in your life.

Place the beet, onion, sweet potatoes, carrots, parsnips, and squash into the bowl of a 6-quart slow cooker. Add the orange juice, duck sauce, salt, thyme, and rosemary. Toss with a wooden spoon to combine. Cover the slow cooker and cook on high for 4½ hours.

Transfer to a serving bowl.

DESSERTS

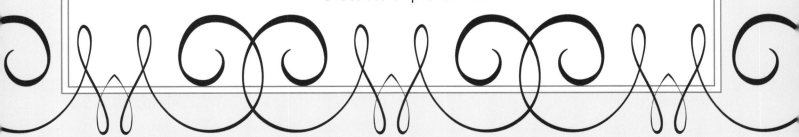

Chocolate Mousse Pie

DAIRY OR PARVE ▪ MAKES 10 SERVINGS ▪ NON-GEBROKTS

nonstick cooking spray

6 tablespoons sugar, divided

12 ounces good-quality semisweet chocolate, chopped

1 cup (2 sticks) unsalted butter or margarine

4 teaspoons vanilla extract

¼ teaspoon fine sea salt

6 large eggs, separated

Chocoholics beware, this one is dangerous and will satisfy even the deepest cravings. This recipe starts with my mother-in-law's famous chocolate mousse and bakes some of it to form a dense, luscious cake base which falls and is then filled with the remaining velvety mousse.

As with any dish using raw eggs, this is not suitable for the very young or people with compromised immune systems, due to the risk of salmonella. If you are worried about this issue, since some of the mousse in this recipe does not get cooked, try to find pasteurized eggs.

Preheat oven to 350°F.

Spray a 9-inch springform pan with a heavy coating of nonstick cooking spray. Sprinkle with 1 tablespoon sugar, tapping the sides to distribute it evenly over the bottom and a little bit on the sides. Set aside.

Set a metal bowl over a pot of barely simmering water to form a double boiler. Melt the chocolate, butter or margarine, and 3 tablespoons sugar in the bowl, stirring occasionally. When completely smooth, remove from heat and stir in vanilla and salt.

Meanwhile, beat the egg whites until soft peaks form, about 2 minutes on medium-high. Gradually add 2 tablespoons sugar and continue to beat until stiff peaks form, about 3–4 minutes. Set aside.

Beat the egg yolks until thick and lemon-colored.

When the chocolate is ready, mix a large spoonful of the warm chocolate into the yolks to temper them and keep them from scrambling. Then, transfer all the yolks into the chocolate mixture, stirring until smooth.

Fold a large dollop of the egg whites into the chocolate mixture, then gently fold in the remaining egg whites.

Pour 3 cups of the mousse mixture into the prepared pan and bake for 25 minutes, until set. Store remaining mousse in refrigerator.

Place the cake immediately from the oven into the refrigerator for 20 minutes. Then, pour remaining mousse into the slightly fallen center. Use a small metal offset spatula to spread it evenly over the cake. Refrigerate until ready to serve.

Ebony and Ivory

DAIRY ▪ MAKES 16 SERVINGS ▪ NON-GEBROKTS

15 ounces good-quality semi-sweet or bittersweet chocolate, broken or cut into bits

¾ cup (1½ sticks) sweet butter, cut into small pieces

3 teaspoons instant coffee (not freeze-dried), dissolved in 3 teaspoons water

6 large eggs, separated

3 tablespoons sugar

12 ounces good-quality white chocolate, broken or cut into bits

⅓ cup plus 1 tablespoon water

2 cups heavy cream

This is by far the most requested and beautiful dairy dessert I have ever made. It has two creamy layers, one of chocolate mousse and one of white chocolate mousse. The two sit one atop the other for a most dramatic presentation. It is very easy to make, especially if using a microwave to melt the chocolate. See note about using raw eggs on page 220.

My husband teases me that my baking pantry looks more like a plumber's tool box because one of my most valuable possessions is a propane torch. I use it in this recipe to release the sides of the pan. A hot towel also does the trick. If you are going to buy a propane torch, get the small, hand-held version used for baking. I have come close to melting the countertop on too many occasions to count with my full-size model.

Ebony Mousse Layer: Melt the chocolate and butter together in a bowl over a pot of simmering hot water or in a microwave on MEDIUM (50%) for about 2–3 minutes. Stir to hasten the melting and to smooth the mixture. Remove from microwave or stovetop and whisk in the dissolved coffee powder and egg yolks. Set aside.

In a clean dry bowl, beat the egg whites at medium speed until soft peaks form. Slowly sprinkle in the sugar, beating on high until stiff but not dry.

Fold the egg whites into the chocolate mixture until completely incorporated.

Using a spatula, scrape the mousse into a 10-inch springform pan, being careful to keep the top half of the pan clean. Place in refrigerator.

Ivory Mousse Layer: Melt the white chocolate and water in a bowl over a pot of simmering hot water or in a microwave on LOW (30%) for about 2 minutes. Stir to hasten the melting and to smooth the mixture. Make sure the chocolate is completely smooth or the mousse will taste grainy.

Whip the cream until soft peaks form, not too stiff. Carefully fold the cream into the melted white chocolate until completely incorporated.

Remove the pan from the refrigerator and immediately turn the ivory mousse on top of the ebony layer. Use a metal spatula to level the top perfectly with the rim of the pan. Don't manipulate for too long because the white mousse starts to set quickly.

Refrigerate for 4–6 hours before unmolding. This dessert can be made two days in advance and refrigerated covered in the pan, or frozen for up to a month.

Before unmolding the dessert, warm the sides of the springform pan ring with a hot, wet, wrung-out towel or a propane torch. Release the sides of the pan. Smooth sides with a metal spatula if necessary for a cleaner look. This can also be done in individual servings as pictured.

Lemon Mousse Parfaits

DAIRY OR PARVE ▪ **MAKES 6 SERVINGS** ▪ **NON-GEBROKTS**

¾ cup sugar

1 tablespoon potato starch

2 large eggs

3 large egg yolks

zest of 2 lemons (yellow part only, not the white pith)

juice of 3 lemons

1 cup heavy cream or nondairy whipping cream

½ cup confectioner's sugar

blueberries or raspberries

For a light, ethereal ending to a meal, try this lemon mousse. The lemon color and flavor are both complemented by the fresh berries. In this recipe, homemade lemon curd is transformed into mousse with whipped cream.

Combine the sugar and potato starch in a heavy medium-sized pot. Whisk in the eggs, egg yolks, lemon zest, and lemon juice until blended.

Turn the heat to medium and cook the mixture, whisking continuously, until it is thick and bubbly, about 3–4 minutes. Whisk for 1 minute longer. Remove from the heat.

Place a strainer over a medium bowl. Pour the lemon mixture through the strainer, using your whisk to push it through. The zest and egg solids will get caught in the strainer and should be discarded.

Lay a sheet of plastic wrap directly on the lemon curd, touching the surface so that it does not form a skin. Place in the freezer to quickly cool while you whip the cream.

In the bowl of an electric stand mixer, beat the cream on high speed until it is thick and stiff peaks form. Slowly beat in the confectioner's sugar until it is all incorporated.

Remove the lemon curd from the freezer. Using a spatula, fold in one-third of the whipped cream to lighten the mixture. Fold in remaining cream until it is an even, pale-yellow color. Refrigerate until needed.

Put a handful of blueberries or raspberries into each of 6 wine glasses or other stemmed glasses. Top with lemon mousse. Serve chilled.

No-Bake Giant Napoleon Cake

DAIRY OR PARVE ▪ MAKES 12 SERVINGS ▪ GEBROKTS

butter or margarine,
   for greasing

2 (3.4-ounce) boxes instant
   vanilla pudding and pie
   filling

2½ cups milk or nondairy
   creamer

1 cup heavy cream or
   nondairy whipping cream

1 (10-ounce) box whole
   matzo boards

3 ounces good-quality
   semi-sweet chocolate,
   broken into ½-inch pieces

⅔ cup honey

This dessert is a quick and easy no-bake pudding cake. The layers get creamier the longer it sits in the refrigerator.

With butter or margarine, lightly grease a 9- by 13-inch baking pan. Set aside.

In a medium bowl, whisk the pudding mix with milk or creamer until thoroughly blended.

In the bowl of a stand mixer, on medium-high speed, beat the whipping cream until thick and stiff peaks form, about 5 minutes.

Fold the whipped cream into the pudding mixture.

Arrange a single layer of matzo sheets in the prepared pan, breaking to fit as needed. Top with half the pudding mixture. Use an offset spatula to spread evenly over the matzo.

Top with a second layer of matzo. Add the remaining pudding, spreading with the offset spatula. Top with a layer of matzo.

Place the chopped chocolate and honey into a microwave-safe bowl. Microwave on high power for 30 seconds. Stir until smooth and melted.

Pour the glaze over the top layer of matzo. Use the offset spatula to spread evenly.

Place into the refrigerator, uncovered, or without allowing the cover to touch the chocolate. Allow to fully chill and set. This can be made a day or two in advance.

Butterscotch Crunch Bars

DAIRY OR PARVE ▪ MAKES 20 BARS ▪ GEBROKTS

Preheat oven to 350°F.

Melt the butter or margarine and brown sugar in a pot over medium heat, whisking until the mixture is melted and smooth.

Cover a jelly-roll pan with aluminum foil. Line the pan with a single layer of matzo, breaking as necessary to fit. Pour the brown sugar mixture over the matzos, spreading evenly with an offset spatula to make sure every surface is covered. Bake for 10 minutes.

In a medium bowl, toss the pecans, coconut, chocolate chips, and cranberries.

When you remove the pan from the oven, sprinkle an even layer of the coconut mixture over the top. Cut into bars while warm.

12 tablespoons butter or margarine

½ cup dark brown sugar

4 matzo boards

1 cup chopped pecans

1 cup shredded sweetened coconut

½ cup semi-sweet chocolate chips

⅓ cups sweetened dried cranberries

Melon Granitas

PARVE ▪ MAKES 10-12 SERVINGS ▪ NON-GEBROKTS

1 cup sugar

½ cup water

3-4 pounds ripe, seedless watermelon, honeydew, or cantaloupe

½ bunch mint leaves, stems discarded

fresh mint leaves for garnish

The sugar water that you make for this recipe is really a simple syrup. It is wonderful to flavor teas or as the base for lemonade. The ratio is always 2:1, so feel free to make a larger batch than specified below and store the remainder in your refrigerator.

Serve granitas in clear glasses so you can see the beautiful, glittering ice crystals.

You can also make espresso granitas by following the same procedure and substituting 3 cups cooled espresso or coffee for the watermelon juice and garnishing with a dollop of whipped cream.

Place the sugar and water into a small pot. Bring to a boil and cook for 2 minutes. Remove from heat and cool completely to room temperature.

Remove the rind from the watermelon or other melon and discard. Chop the flesh into 1½-inch chunks. Purée the melon in a blender, in batches if necessary, until smooth. Strain through a mesh sieve into a large bowl and discard the pulp. You should have 4 cups melon juice. Add ⅓ cup of the prepared sugar-water to the melon juice. You will have extra sugar-water for another use.

Pour the mixture into a large, shallow, non-reactive pan, like glass or stainless steel; aluminum will react with the fruit acids and leave a metallic taste in the granita. The larger and shallower the pan, the larger the surface area will be and the granita will freeze more quickly. Just make sure it fits comfortably in your freezer so the mixture doesn't spill. Cover with plastic wrap. Place into the freezer. Stir and scrape with a fork every 30 minutes. Be sure to scrape ice crystals off the sides and into the middle of the pan, until too frozen to stir, between 3–4 hours.

Put mint and ¼ cup of the remaining sugar-water into blender and purée until smooth.

When mixture is frozen solid, scrape with the tines of a fork, pulling the mixture in rows towards you to make the mixture fluffy, with large ice crystals. If too frozen to scrape, leave at room temperature for 10 minutes. Place crystals into serving glasses. Garnish the granitas with a drizzle of the mint syrup and a fresh mint leaf.

White Chocolate Mousse in Chocolate Boxes

DAIRY ▪ MAKES 4 SERVINGS ▪ NON-GEBROKTS

WHITE CHOCOLATE MOUSSE:

- 8 ounces good-quality white chocolate, broken into small pieces
- 1 cup heavy cream
- 6 tablespoons confectioner's sugar

CHOCOLATE BOXES:

- 6 (4-ounce) milk chocolate bars

Most chocolate bars have indentations or score marks. Use these as guides to help break your chocolate into 4 even squares from which to build your box.

Place the white chocolate in a microwave-safe bowl. Microwave for 45 seconds. Stir with a silicone spatula. Return the bowl to the microwave and microwave for 30–35 seconds more. When you remove the bowl and stir again, it should be all melted. Let the chocolate cool for 5 minutes.

If your mixer has a whisk attachment, use it here. Place the heavy cream and confectioner's sugar into the bowl of a mixer. Beat at high speed until it is whipped, fluffy, and stiff. When you run a spatula through the center, it should leave a mark. If it doesn't, whip it a little longer.

With a spatula, scoop the white chocolate into the cream. Beat it in with the mixer for 10 seconds. Place the bowl into the refrigerator.

Make your chocolate boxes: Break each milk chocolate bar so that you have 4 equal square walls (the number of squares will depend on your chocolate bar).

Take two of the extra squares (or 2 tablespoons of chocolate chips, if you have no extra squares) and place them into a microwave-safe bowl. Microwave for 60 seconds. Stir with a silicone spatula. Return the bowl to the microwave and microwave for 30–35 seconds more. When you remove and stir it again, it should be all melted.

Carefully remove the melted chocolate. Build chocolate boxes on a plate so that you can easily move them to the refrigerator. With a paintbrush, use the melted chocolate as the "glue" to attach the 4 chocolate walls together to make a box. Make sure the smooth sides are facing in. Repeat with remaining chocolate bars. Place the boxes in the refrigerator to firm up for 5 minutes.

Fill each chocolate box with the white chocolate mousse.

Hold some of the extra chocolate over the top of the mousse. Run a vegetable peeler over the chocolate to make shavings that fall onto the mousse.

Lemon Meringues

PARVE ▪ MAKES 6 SERVINGS ▪ NON-GEBROKTS

MERINGUES:

2 egg whites

pinch of fine sea salt

½ cup sugar, super-fine if possible

½ teaspoon vanilla extract

¼ teaspoon almond extract

LEMON CREAM:

1½ cups sugar

⅓ cup potato starch

2 cups water

⅓ cup plus 3 tablespoons lemon juice, divided

3 egg yolks

GARNISHES:

¼ cup nondairy whipping cream

2 ounces semi-sweet chocolate

1 teaspoon margarine

6 hazelnuts or cashews

This is a fabulous Passover dessert. The three components — meringues, lemon cream, and chocolate-dipped nuts can all be prepared 2–3 days in advance and assembled right before serving. Try using dairy whipping cream and white chocolate-dipped nuts — for dairy meals.

Allow the egg whites to stand at room temperature for 30 minutes. If you are short on time, place the egg whites in a stainless steel bowl and set it in a bowl of warm water for 2 minutes to bring the whites to room temperature quickly.

Cover two baking sheets with parchment paper. Preheat oven to the lowest possible temperature, about 175°F.

Place the egg whites in the bowl of a mixer. With the whisk attachment, whip the egg whites with the salt about 5 minutes or until soft peaks form; the tips will curl. Gradually add the sugar, beating on high until stiff peaks form; the tips will stand straight and sugar will be dissolved. Fold in vanilla and almond extracts.

Evenly spread the meringues to form 12 circles on the parchment-paper lined baking sheets. Flatten slightly so they have a diameter of about 3- to 4-inches. Place the two baking sheets in the oven for 4 hours. When they are done, remove from the parchment; if the bottoms are sticky in the center, return them to the oven for longer. You want them completely dried out but not browned. Transfer to a wire rack to cool.

When completely cool, place in an airtight, covered container. Store at room temperature for up to 3 days.

Lemon Cream: In a medium saucepan, combine the sugar and potato starch. Whisk in the water, stirring constantly, until the mixture comes to a boil over medium-high heat. Boil for 1 minute. Remove from heat. Stir in ⅓ cup lemon juice.

In a small bowl, stir the egg yolks with a fork. Add a spoonful of the lemon cream to the eggs. Slowly stir the egg mixture into the lemon cream. Continue to cook for 1 minute. Stir in remaining 3 tablespoons of lemon juice. Remove from heat. Cool for 15 minutes. Cover the top of the filling with plastic wrap, making sure it touches the cream, or a skin will form. Cool to room temperature or refrigerate overnight or up to 2 days in advance.

Garnishes: In a large bowl, with mixer at a high speed, whip the whipping cream. Reserve for a whipped cream dollop on top.

Over a double boiler or in a microwave, melt the chocolate with the margarine. Roll each nut in the chocolate and gently remove with a fork to a sheet of wax paper. Let stand until chocolate is set and shiny; can be put in refrigerator for 5 minutes. Store in an airtight container until ready for use.

To assemble, spread half the meringues with lemon cream. Top with remaining meringues. Place a small dollop of whipped cream on the top of each "sandwich" and top with a chocolate-dipped hazelnut or cashew. Serve immediately.

Best-Ever Sponge Cake

PARVE ▪ MAKES 10-12 SERVINGS ▪ GEBROKTS

2 large lemons
9 large eggs, separated
2 cups sugar
¼ cup club soda
½ cup potato starch
½ cup matzo cake meal

The week before Passover had arrived, and Sylvia and her husband Hymie were to be guests at their son and daughter-in-law's home for the holiday. She called her daughter-in-law and said, "Please let me make something to help you out." Not wanting to burden her elderly mother-in-law, she replied, "Nothing, Ma, just come." Sylvia would not take no for an answer and insisted on making her special sponge cake. On Erev Yom Tov, Sylvia and Hymie drove up to their son and daughter-in-law's house and everyone helped unpack their loaded car. When the car was emptied, the daughter-in-law asked, "Ma, where is the sponge cake?" To which Sylvia replied, "Oh, it is a funny story. I made the cake and it smelled so delicious that we had to have a little sample. So I took a little piece, and Hymie had a little piece, and I had a sliver, and Hymie had a little sliver, and before we knew it the whole cake was gone." Later that evening while cleaning up in the kitchen, the daughter-in-law asked Hymie, "So Dad, how was the sponge cake?" To which he said, "Sponge cake, vhat sponge cake, der vas no sponge cake." Sylvia had eaten the whole thing all by herself!

Although the method of rebeating the egg whites seems unusual, it really does work. So don't be alarmed by the instructions that call for it. This cake can easily be transformed into a delicious dairy strawberry shortcake. Just cut it in half and fill with fresh whipped cream and strawberries.

Preheat oven to 350°F.

Using a microplane, zest 2 teaspoons of lemon peel from the lemons, making sure to get only the yellow part, not the bitter white pith. Set aside. Cut the lemons and squeeze ¼ cup of lemon juice. Set aside.

Beat the egg whites until stiff; set aside. In a separate bowl, beat the egg yolks, sugar, club soda, and reserved lemon juice for 3 minutes on medium-high speed. Gradually add the potato starch and matzo cake meal.

Using a rubber spatula, fold the whites into the yolk mixture. Add the lemon zest. Beat for 2 minutes. Pour into an ungreased tube pan. Bake for 1 hour and 10 minutes. Invert until completely cool. Run a knife around the cake and remove from pan.

Giant Zebra Fudge Cookies

PARVE ▪ MAKES 18 LARGE COOKIES ▪ GEBROKTS

I do many cooking demonstrations all over the country and each one is wonderful and memorable. One last year was for Kimpitorin Aid, which helps new mothers. The hostess, Goldie Stern, set the event in a tent decorated with lights, white paper balls from the ceiling, vines, trees, and berries. She coordinated the look down to pieces of tree trunk to hold the platters. So there I was in this gorgeous environment, prepared to cook and teach about fabulous food, MY fabulous food, and all I heard were murmurings about an awesome cookie that Goldie's sister-in-law, Zipporah Farkas, had made for the event.

Guests kept gravitating over to the cookie table, whispering to their neighbors about these cookies. Well, I have to say, I had never been upstaged by a cookie before, but it clearly happened that night. I felt that the only appropriate payback was for Zipporah to give me the recipe to use in this book. She was adorable and obliged. She credits it to her friend Rivki Shaulson. I guess if I have to share the spotlight with a cookie, I'm glad it is such a pretty, yummy, fudgy one.

½ cup vegetable oil

2 cups sugar

2 cups matzo meal

1 cup good-quality Dutch process cocoa powder

4 large eggs

1 teaspoon vanilla extract

2 teaspoons baking powder

confectioner's sugar, sifted

Preheat oven to 350°F.

Line 2 large cookie sheets or jelly-roll pans with parchment paper. Set aside.

In the bowl of an electric stand mixer, mix the oil, sugar, matzo meal, cocoa powder, eggs, vanilla, and baking powder until a soft dough forms.

Roll the dough into 18 balls slightly larger than golf balls.

Fill a small bowl with confectioner's sugar and stir with a fork to break up any clumps. Lower the balls, one at a time, into confectioner's sugar and toss to coat heavily and completely. Transfer to prepared pans. Leave room between the dough balls, as the cookies spread during baking.

Bake for 18 minutes. If you like, you can make smaller cookies; form walnut-sized balls and bake for 12 minutes.

Cool completely.

Grandma Mollie's Compote

PARVE ▪ MAKES 25 SERVINGS ▪ NON-GEBROKTS

7 pounds large dried plums (prunes)

1½ pounds dried apricots

3 lemons, sliced

3 generous cups sugar

Compote was one of my grandmother's specialties. If someone mentioned that they liked it, she would rush into her kitchen and whip up pounds and pounds for distribution. One afternoon, there was a knock on my husband and father-in-law's office door. They opened it to find Grandma Mollie lugging a wagon twice her size, full of compote jars. She had taken a bus and two subways, but like the postal system, neither rain nor snow could keep Mollie from her compote deliveries.

Make sure you use a very large pot to give the liquid space to simmer. You can add dried pears or nectarines to the compote as well. In the summer, Grandma Mollie substituted fresh peeled peaches and whole cherries with their stems removed, for the prunes and apricots. The results were divine. Store the compote in a covered jar or container for up to 2–3 weeks in the refrigerator.

Place the prunes, apricots, and lemons into a large pot. Sprinkle in the sugar. Add water to cover by 3 inches. Bring to a low boil. Reduce heat to a low simmer. Cover the pot.

Cook at a low simmer for 3 hours. Serve in dessert or martini glasses; hang a spiral of lemon zest off the side of each cup.

Chocolate Truffles

DAIRY OR PARVE ▪ MAKES 30-36 TRUFFLES ▪ NON-GEBROKTS

People think of truffles as such a luxurious item, yet they couldn't be easier to make. Pop one in your mouth for a mid-afternoon snack or serve as a small delicious bite at the end of a large meal. There is so much buzz out there lately about the good effects of chocolate — hey, think of it as health food!

Finely chop the chocolate by hand or in a food processor fitted with a metal blade, and place in a medium bowl. Pour the cream into a small heavy saucepan. Bring to a rolling boil over medium heat. Pour the cream over the chocolate. With a wooden spoon, gently stir to melt the chocolate. Don't whisk or stir too strongly or you will incorporate air. Cover. Chill until firm, about 2 hours.

Line a baking sheet with parchment or waxed paper. With a small melon baller or ice-cream scoop, drop mixture by rounded teaspoonfuls onto prepared sheet. Freeze until firm, about 20 minutes.

Place the cocoa, confectioner's sugar, and chopped nuts into 3 separate shallow bowls.

Roll ⅓ of the balls into the cocoa mixture, ⅓ into the confectioner's sugar, and ⅓ into the chopped nuts. Quickly roll between your palms to form them into a perfect round shape. You may need to re-roll in the nuts or sugar if too much falls off. Return to parchment-lined baking sheet or other parchment-lined container, in a single layer. Cover with plastic and chill until ready to serve. Can be made 10 days ahead; keep refrigerated.

12 ounces good-quality semi-sweet or bittersweet chocolate

⅔ cup heavy cream or nondairy whipping cream

2 tablespoons Dutch processed cocoa powder

2 tablespoons confectioner's sugar

3 tablespoons finely chopped unsalted pistachios, almonds, or hazelnuts

Jelly Thumbprint Cookies

DAIRY OR PARVE ■ MAKES 30 COOKIES ■ GEBROKTS

1 cup sugar

1 cup (2 sticks) butter or margarine

3 large egg yolks

zest of 1 large lemon

1¼ cups matzo cake meal

¾ cup potato starch

¼ teaspoon fine sea salt

sugar

jam, flavor of your choice

You can use any flavor jam to fill in the thumbprint, although apricot is my favorite. You can use the same dough, leaving out the lemon zest, and stick chocolate chips into the thumbprint instead of jam for a chocolate-studded spin on this cookie.

Preheat oven to 350°F.

Cover 2 cookie sheets with parchment paper. Set aside.

In the bowl of a stand mixer, beat the sugar and butter or margarine until creamy. Add the egg yolks. Beat in the lemon zest.

Sprinkle in the cake meal, potato starch, and salt. Mix until blended.

Place about ½ cup sugar into a small bowl. Using a tablespoon measure, drop rounded spoonfuls of dough into the sugar. Shake the bowl so the dough gets coated with sugar. Re-roll into balls and drop onto prepared sheet. Leave room between cookies for spreading. When you have a full sheet, use your thumb to make an indentation on the center of each cookie. Fill with ¼ teaspoon of jam.

Bake for 12 minutes. Allow to cool completely. Use a thin-bladed spatula to remove cookies.

Sorbet Ruffles

DAIRY OR PARVE ▪ MAKES 16 SERVINGS ▪ NON-GEBROKTS

1 pint raspberry sorbet

1 pint vanilla ice-cream, can be parve

1 pint mango, passion fruit, or lemon sorbet

16 (2½-inch) pleated paper baking cups (muffin sized)

dessert sauces (see note above) or chocolate syrup

16 raspberries

No time to bake? Been in the kitchen too long? Here's the perfect answer. A gorgeous little layered ruffle of sorbet and ice-cream. A perfect light end to a big meal.

One of my favorite food finds was a gift from Barbara Strashun. She was my wonderful tour guide when I did a cooking show at the Viking Culinary Arts Center for her school in St. Louis. On our way to the airport we detoured to a food warehouse for these goodies. They are squeeze bottles of incredible parve dessert sauces in chocolate, vanilla, kiwi, mango, and raspberry. If you don't have these for Passover, chocolate syrup works fine, too. If you have silicone muffin cups, use them. They work great.

Let the sorbets and the ice-cream sit at room temperature for 15 minutes to soften. Transfer the sorbets and ice-cream to bowls to better stir them and make them spreadable.

Place the muffin cups into metal muffin tins. If you don't have muffin tins, create a double thickness of the paper muffin cups and place them into a metal baking pan so that they support each other.

Spread an even layer of raspberry sorbet into the bottom third of each cup. Place into the freezer for 15 minutes. Remove from freezer and spread dollops of vanilla ice-cream to evenly cover the raspberry layer and come up to the second third of the cup. Return to the freezer for 15 minutes. Repeat procedure with the mango sorbet. Cover the pan with plastic wrap. Freeze overnight. Can be made 4 days ahead; keep frozen.

When ready to serve, invert each sorbet cup onto a dessert plate. Remove muffin cup. Decorate plate with desired sauce. Top each with a fresh raspberry.

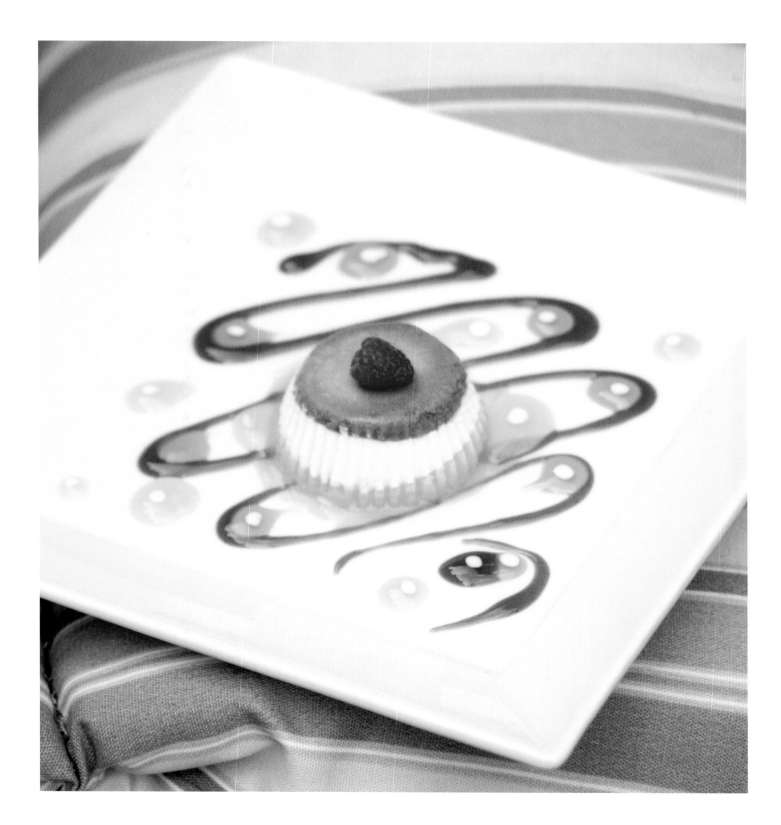

Praline Strips

DAIRY OR PARVE ▪ MAKES 3-4 SERVINGS ▪ GEBROKTS

butter or margarine,
    for greasing

3-4 whole matzo boards

1 cup (2 sticks) unsalted
    butter or margarine

1 cup dark brown sugar

12 ounces chocolate chips or
    chopped chocolate bars

1 cup finely chopped pecans
    or chopped almonds

A friend gave me a great recipe similar to this one for use during the year. The pralines had a graham cracker base. I tried the recipe substituting matzo and was thrilled with the results, as was anyone who stopped by my house that day in December all those years ago when I was working on Passover recipes. As you can imagine, I had to beg them to taste my Passover desserts, since they are not usually craved out of season. I will say, however, that almost everyone asked for a goody bag "to go" of this winner!

Preheat oven to 325°F.

Cover a large cookie sheet with aluminum foil. (I like to use a disposable sheet, as the sheet gets very sticky and messy.)

Grease the foil with butter or margarine. Lay the matzos in a single layer, breaking as needed, to fill the sheet completely. Set aside.

In a large saucepan, melt the butter or margarine over medium-low heat. Add the brown sugar; boil for 5 minutes, stirring constantly. Watch carefully to make sure it doesn't boil over.

Pour the brown sugar mixture over the matzos, spreading evenly. Bake for 8–10 minutes. Turn the oven off. Remove the pan and sprinkle the chocolate over the matzos. Place it back in the oven for another 8 minutes.

Remove from the oven and spread the chocolate in an even layer. Sprinkle with the chopped pecans or almonds. Refrigerate for 1 hour. Break into pieces. Store in an airtight container in the refrigerator.

Unbelievable Brownies

PARVE ▪ MAKES 18 BROWNIES ▪ NON-GEBROKTS

If you love fudgy brownies, you have just hit the jackpot. No one will ever know these are for Passover. Make sure you keep generous amounts of the ingredients on hand. You will definitely be asked for more once you've served your first batch. If you like cakey brownies, you can use ¾ cup matzo cake meal plus ¼ cup potato starch in place of the 1 cup potato starch; note that the recipe will then become gebrokts.

Preheat oven to 350°F.

Spray an 11- by 7-inch brownie pan with nonstick cooking spray. Set aside.

In the bowl of an electric mixer, beat the eggs and sugar until smooth. Add the oil and salt. Mix. Sprinkle in the cocoa powder and mix to make the batter chocolaty. Add the potato starch and mix to combine. Scrape down the sides with a spatula. Stir in the chocolate chips if using.

Pour into prepared pan. Bake for 35–40 minutes. Allow to cool before serving.

nonstick cooking spray

4 large eggs

2 cups sugar

1 cup vegetable oil

½ teaspoon fine sea salt

¾ cup Dutch process cocoa powder

1 cup potato starch

½ cup semi-sweet chocolate chips (optional)

Honey-Chocolate Chip Cookies

PARVE ▪ MAKES 3 DOZEN ▪ GEBROKTS

1 (12-ounce) box Passover honey cake mix

1 tablespoon instant coffee granules

1 cup chopped walnuts

1 large egg

2 tablespoons oil, plus enough orange juice to total ½ cup

1 cup chocolate chips

Preheat oven to 325°F.

Line 2 cookie sheets with parchment paper or lightly grease them. In a medium bowl, combine the dry cake mix, instant coffee, and walnuts.

In a separate bowl, mix the egg with the oil/orange juice mixture. Add the dry ingredients into the egg mixture. Stir in the chocolate chips.

Scoop the dough by rounded teaspoonfuls onto the prepared cookie sheets. Bake 10–15 minutes. Remove to a rack to cool completely.

Chocolate Sorbet

PARVE ▪ MAKES 8 SERVINGS ▪ NON-GEBROKTS

1 cup sugar

2 cups water

½ cup cocoa, good-quality Dutch processed preferred

4 ounces good-quality semi-sweet or bittersweet chocolate (not chocolate chips), broken into chunks

This cool and refreshing dessert is so simple yet so delicious.

Prepare a large pan or bowl of ice water (ice cubes and water). Set aside.

Combine the 1 cup sugar and 2 cups water in a medium saucepan. Bring to a boil. Remove from heat and whisk in the cocoa and the chocolate. Stir until smooth.

Return the saucepan to the heat and bring to a boil again. As soon as bubbles start to appear, remove from heat and set into the prepared pan of ice water.

Cool for 10 minutes. Pour sorbet into an airtight container. Cover and freeze for 3 hours.

Remove from freezer and transfer to a mixing bowl. With a mixer at medium-high speed, beat the mixture for 1 full minute. Return to the container. Cover and place back into the freezer for 3 more hours. Repeat the beating 2 more times during these 3 hours. Freeze until ready to serve.

Serve in small scoops in martini glasses.

Flourless Chocolate Torte

DAIRY OR PARVE ▪ MAKES 10 SERVINGS ▪ NON-GEBROKTS

Dense, thick, chocolaty goodness! Slice it thin — it is decadent.

Preheat oven to 350°F.

Lightly coat a 9-inch springform pan with nonstick cooking spray.

Crack the eggs into a small glass or metal bowl. Place them on the stovetop, but not over a direct flame. You want to warm the eggs, but not cook them. This will allow the eggs to triple in volume when beaten. Set aside.

In a medium pot, melt the chocolates, water, 1 cup sugar, and butter or margarine over medium heat, stirring with a spoon. Remove from heat. Let cool.

Transfer the eggs to a mixing bowl. Add the remaining ⅓ cup sugar to the eggs and beat until tripled in volume. With a rubber spatula, fold the chocolate mixture into the eggs.

Pour into prepared pan. Bake 30–35 minutes; it will be a little loose in center. Serve warm or at room temperature with whipped cream and raspberries.

nonstick cooking spray

5 large eggs

8 ounces unsweetened chocolate

4 ounces best-quality semi-sweet chocolate

½ cup water

1⅓ cups sugar, divided

1 cup (2 sticks) butter or margarine

whipped cream or parve whipped cream, for garnish

raspberries, for garnish

Pineapple Truffles

PARVE ▪ MAKES 50-60 TRUFFLES ▪ NON-GEBROKTS

1¼ cups firmly packed sweetened flaked coconut, divided

¾ cup sugar, divided

1 medium pineapple, ripe

¾ cup confectioner's sugar

4 large egg yolks

Two years before I was asked to teach a class at De Gustibus Cooking School in Macy's Times Square, I did the backroom kitchen work for two different chef friends who were teaching there. The head assistant, Amaral Ozeias, who during his long tenure has seen every great chef and TV personality pass through the doors of that kitchen, quietly motioned for me to come into his office. He pulled out the prettiest little yellow truffle and proceeded to recite the recipe, one of his all-time favorites. This kind gesture was the most delicious favor he could have done for me.

In a blender or food processor fitted with a metal blade, process ¼ cup coconut with ¼ cup sugar. Remove to a bowl or ziplock bag. Set aside.

Cut the pineapple out of the shell. Discard core and cut the flesh into chunks. Purée pineapple in blender or food processor. Transfer the puréed pineapple to a medium pot. Mix in 1 cup coconut, ½ cup sugar, and the confectioner's sugar. Bring to a boil over medium heat. Cook until all the liquid evaporates, about 30–35 minutes, stirring often to make sure the mixture is not browning on the bottom. If the mixture starts to brown, lower heat slightly and stir more often. The mixture will turn a dark golden color. Turn off the heat.

Remove ½ cup of the pineapple mixture and mix it into the egg yolks to temper them. Add the tempered yolks into the pot. At medium-high heat, continue to cook until dry and pulling away from the sides of the pot, about 5 minutes.

Place the pot in the freezer and chill completely.

Remove the pineapple mixture from the freezer. Using a tiny melon baller or ¼ teaspoon measure, make balls. Roll in the coconut/sugar that was blended in the first step. If the truffles get too sticky to roll, place the mixture back into the freezer for a few minutes.

Place on parchment-lined baking sheets and place into freezer. Once frozen, remove and store in an airtight container in single layers separated by parchment paper. Return truffles to freezer.

Serve right from the freezer or place in little paper candy cups or on a platter 10 minutes before serving.

Crumb Cake

DAIRY OR PARVE ▪ MAKES 12 SERVINGS ▪ NON-GEBROKTS

nonstick cooking spray

1 cup sugar

1 cup brown sugar

1 teaspoon baking powder

1 tablespoon vanilla sugar

1 cup vegetable oil

4 large eggs

1 cup potato starch

CRUMB TOPPING:

2 teaspoons ground cinnamon

4 tablespoons (½ stick) butter or margarine, cut into small bits

½ (8-ounce) box ladyfingers, crushed and crumbled

¼ cup brown sugar

¼ cup sugar

When my friend Limor Decter heard I was doing a Passover cookbook, she immediately forwarded me a file of Pesach recipes from her friend Tsippy Nussbaum, who loves Passover food. Tsippy was kind enough to allow me to include this recipe, her favorite of the bunch. The ladyfingers that she recommends are from an 8-ounce box; they are non-gebrokts and made by Oberlander. If you can't find them, you can use another kind of Passover boxed cookie. I used a whole (2.25–ounce) box of Lieber's brand Sugar-Coated Egg Kichel and the recipe worked out fine.

Preheat oven to 350°F.

Spray a 9- by- 13-inch baking pan with nonstick cooking spray. Set aside.

In the bowl of a stand mixer, at medium speed, mix the sugar, brown sugar, baking powder, vanilla sugar, oil, eggs, and potato starch until you have a smooth batter.

Pour into prepared pan and bake, uncovered, for 20 minutes.

In a medium bowl, toss the cinnamon, butter or margarine, crushed ladyfingers, brown sugar, and sugar. Use your fingers to pinch into coarse crumbs.

Sprinkle the crumbs on top of the cake and return to the oven to bake for an additional 35 minutes.

Fresh Fruit Lollipops

PARVE ▪ NUMBER OF SERVINGS WILL VARY ▪ NON-GEBROKTS

blueberries

raspberries

green and red grapes

honeydew, peeled, cut into ¾-inch thick slices

cantaloupe, peeled, cut into ¾-inch thick slices

watermelon, peeled, cut into ¾-inch thick slices

kiwi, sliced into ¾-inch thick slices

lollipop sticks or skewers

medium-sized round cookie cutters

mini-sized assorted cookie cutters

Your guests will love and appreciate this beautiful and low-fat dessert option. When presented in such a pretty way, no one will feel like they are sacrificing if they only go for the fruit. This recipe is more of a concept than a recipe. Use whatever fruits you have on hand that are just ripe. If your fruit is overripe you will have a hard time threading it. Be creative with your shapes. There are thousands of cookie cutters out there in all shapes and sizes, so the only limit is your imagination.

Thread the skewers with blueberries, raspberries, and grapes or alternate any two or three of these, leaving the top 4 inches bare.

Using the medium-sized round cookie cutter, cut out the desired shape from any of the honeydew, cantaloupe, or watermelon slices. Using the mini cookie cutters, cut a hole in the center of each shape. Using the same mini cookie cutter, cut that shape out of a different-colored melon or kiwi slice. Set that shape into the hole. Thread the lollipop stick or skewer through both, making sure it goes through both fruits and back into the top of the first fruit for stability.

Continue until all the fruit is used.

French Almond Macaroons

PARVE ▪ MAKES 24 COOKIES ▪ NON-GEBROKTS

1½ cups sugar

1¼ cups blanched slivered
   almonds

¼ cup potato starch

3 large egg whites

pinch of fine sea salt

1½ teaspoons almond extract

Although I'm a big fan of the can, macaroons mean different things to different people. Yes, the can on Passover means mounds of chewy coconut that I do look forward to. However, there is nothing like a French macaroon. These contain no coconut. Instead, they are soft pillows of almond and meringue. Made right, they are the perfect balance between sticky and chewy and are sold at every patisserie in Paris, dressed up in many ways. You can flavor them with liqueurs, sandwich jelly, or chocolate ganache between two cookies, or just drizzle chocolate over the tops. Personally, I love them plain. The recipe is simple; just make sure you whip the egg whites properly so they are stiff but not dry. If your stand mixer has a whisk attachment you should use it. You must use parchment paper to line the cookie sheet or your cookies will stick miserably.

Preheat oven to 325°F.

Line 2 large cookie sheets with parchment paper.

Place the sugar and almonds into the bowl of a food processor fitted with a metal blade. Process for a full 3 minutes so that the almonds are ground to a powder. Add the potato starch and process for 1 minute more. Transfer the almond mixture to a medium bowl. Set aside.

Place the egg whites, salt, and almond extract into the bowl of a stand mixer. Beat on medium-high speed for 2 minutes until stiff peaks form.

With a spatula, fold the almond mixture into the egg whites in 3 parts, using the spatula to fold the egg whites over and over until the almond mixture is incorporated. The batter will be sticky and thick. Allow the batter to rest for 20 minutes.

Spoon the batter by full tablespoons onto the prepared sheets, leaving room for the macaroons to spread as they bake.

Bake 1 sheet at a time for 18–20 minutes or until the cookies are puffed, shiny, and have formed a skin on top.

When the cookies come out of the oven, slide the parchment paper off the hot sheet. The cookies must cool completely before they are removed. You will need a thin metal spatula, as the cookies tend to stick.

Chocolate-Drenched Stuffed Fruit

PARVE ▪ MAKES 6 SERVINGS ▪ NON-GEBROKTS

12 large raspberries

1 tablespoon sweetened, shredded coconut, divided

12 medium-large strawberries

12 large blueberries

2 medium bananas

4 (3.5oz) bars good-quality parve bittersweet Swiss chocolate

12 pecan halves

Line a large cookie sheet with parchment paper. Place a small cooling rack on a small cookie sheet.

Stuff the raspberries with about ¼ teaspoon of coconut, and place them on the cooling rack, coconut side up.

Remove the greens and dig a hole about the size of a blueberry in the tops of the strawberries. Gently press a blueberry to fit deep into each prepared strawberry. Place these on one side of the parchment-lined cookie sheet.

Peel each banana and slice it on the bias into 6 pieces. Place the banana bites on the other side of the parchment-lined cookie sheet.

Fill a medium pot with 2–3 inches of water. Over medium-low heat, bring the water to just simmering (about 175–180°F). Using a serrated knife, chop the chocolate into ½-inch pieces. Reserve about ¼ of the chopped chocolate away from the heat. Place the remaining three-quarters of the chocolate (about 10 ounces) into a large metal bowl and set the bowl over the barely simmering water.

Using a wooden spoon, slowly stir the chocolate often until it is melted, scraping down the sides of the bowl as needed. Do NOT let the water come to a rolling simmer or boil; excessive heat will damage the chocolate. Once all the chocolate is melted, immediately remove the bowl from the heat and add the remaining chopped chocolate. Gently stir until all the chocolate is melted.

Working quickly, drop a banana piece into the chocolate. Without stabbing it, lift it out of the chocolate with a fork. Lightly tap the back of the fork on the edge of the bowl, and then slide it over the edge to remove any excess chocolate. Place the banana back on parchment-lined cookie sheet. Top with a pecan. Repeat with the remaining pieces.

With a firm but gentle grip on the point of a strawberry, dip it into the chocolate about ¾ of the way up, being careful not to lose the blueberry. Place the berry back on the parchment-lined cookie sheet, blueberry side down. Repeat with remaining strawberries.

Using a small spoon, gently drizzle the remaining chocolate over the prepared raspberries.

Place all fruit in the refrigerator; serve well-chilled. Eat within a couple of hours, or store in an air-tight container refrigerated for one day, or in the freezer for up to a week. They are great frozen treats!

Warm Runny Chocolate Soufflés

DAIRY OR PARVE ▪ MAKES 8 SERVINGS ▪ GEBROKTS

nonstick cooking spray

4 ounces good-quality semi-sweet or bittersweet chocolate

½ cup (1 stick) unsalted butter or margarine

4 large eggs

1½ cups sugar, plus more for coating ramekins

¾ cup matzo cake meal

2 tablespoons potato starch

1 teaspoon vanilla extract

Molten chocolate cakes have made a huge splash in restaurants in recent years. I love the idea but I am not always thrilled with the taste or texture. Even after experimenting and trying to develop a recipe for this book, I was not satisfied. When I was about to give up, my food guru and food stylist, Melanie Dubberley, suggested I try using my favorite brownie recipe and just undercook it. I turned to Fishbein Brownies, in our family for generations, beloved by literally hundreds of eaters, and gave the theory a try. Less a molten cake, more of a soufflé, call it what you want, it was spectacular. Here was the chocolate flavor I was looking for and the warm runny center that is the signature of this dessert.

Preheat oven to 450°F.

Generously coat 8 (6.8-ounce) ramekins with nonstick cooking spray, and lightly coat them with granulated sugar. Hold a ramekin on its side. Tap the sides, turning the ramekin to coat the sides with sugar as well. Repeat with remaining ramekins. (If you use larger ramekins you will get fewer servings.)

Break the chocolate into small pieces; place it and the butter or margarine into a small microwave-safe dish. Microwave on medium power for 15-second intervals, stirring between, until the chocolate is completely melted.

In the bowl of an electric stand mixer, beat the eggs on high speed until foamy. Slowly pour in 1½ cups sugar, and continue beating until very fluffy and pale yellow. On low speed, stir in the matzo cake meal, potato starch, and vanilla until thoroughly combined.

Increase speed to high, and while beating, slowly drizzle in the melted chocolate mixture. Once added, beat until all the chocolate is incorporated, about 1 minute.

For ease of pouring, transfer the batter into a large measuring cup. Fill each ramekin halfway. Set the ramekins onto a baking sheet, and bake for 14–15 minutes until the tops are brown and the centers are warm.

(Alternatively, the filled ramekins can be refrigerated. Just leave at room temperature for 30 minutes before baking.)

Serve immediately, being cautious as the ramekins will be hot!

Chocolate Chip Cheesecake

DAIRY ▪ MAKES 12 SERVINGS ▪ GEBROKTS OR NON-GEBROKTS

nonstick cooking spray

1 (10-ounce) can chocolate chip macaroons (about 28 small macaroons)

2 tablespoons butter, melted

3 (8-ounce) bars cream cheese, softened

1 cup sugar

2 large eggs

1 cup sour cream, can use reduced fat but not fat-free

1 tablespoon vanilla

1 cup semisweet chocolate chips

GLAZE:

3 ounces good-quality milk chocolate, broken into small chunks

½ cup heavy whipping cream

Cheesecake tops my list of favorite indulgences. This one is so smooth and creamy and the thick chocolate ganache layer just puts it right over the edge.

This recipe will be gebrokts or nongrebrokts depending on the macaroons you use. Carefully check the ingredients list for matzo meal.

Preheat oven to 350°F.

Spray a 9-inch nonstick springform pan with nonstick cooking spray. Set aside.

Place the macaroons into the bowl of a food processor fitted with a metal blade. Pulse until it forms crumbs. Transfer to a medium bowl. Mix in the melted butter. Press the crumbs into the prepared pan. Set aside.

In the bowl of a stand mixer, beat the cream cheese until fluffy. Add the sugar and eggs, beating until smooth. Beat in the sour cream and vanilla.

Using a spatula, fold in the chocolate chips. Pour the batter onto the prepared crust.

Bake on the center rack, uncovered, for 1 hour. Turn oven off and leave the cake in the oven for an additional hour. Remove from oven and cool completely. It is okay if it has a crack in the center, it will be covered.

Prepare the glaze: Place the chopped chocolate into a medium bowl. Set aside.

Heat the cream in a small pot until simmering. Pour over the chocolate and stir to hasten the melting, until smooth. Using a small offset spatula, spread over the top of the cheesecake. Refrigerate for 4 hours or until ready to serve.

Run a small knife or metal spatula around rim of cake to loosen it. Release the sides of the springform pan.

Index